AFTER
THE DARKEST HOUR

———————

THE SUN WILL SHINE
AGAIN

ELIZABETH MEHREN

Foreword by Rabbi Harold S. Kushner

A FIRESIDE BOOK

Published by Simon & Schuster

AFTER
THE DARKEST HOUR

THE SUN WILL SHINE
AGAIN

*A Parent's Guide
to Coping with the Loss of a Child*

FIRESIDE
Rockefeller Center
1230 Avenue of the Americas
New York, NY 10020

Designed by Lucy Albanese

Manufactured in the United States of America

5 7 9 10 8 6 4

Library of Congress Cataloging-in-Publication Data
Mehren, Elizabeth.
After the darkest hour, the sun will shine again: a parent's guide
to coping with the loss of a child / Elizabeth Mehren;
foreword by Harold S. Kushner.
1. Children—Death—Psychological aspects.
2. Parents—Psychology.
3. Loss (Psychology).
4. Bereavement—Psychological aspects.   I. Title.
BF575.G7M444   1997   97–1391
155.9'37'085—dc21   CIP

ISBN 0-684-81170-7

Permissions appear on page 189.

Acknowledgments

Thank you, dear friends and advisers:

Meg Anderson, Ann Marie Cunningham, Nancy Day, Melissa Everett, Aviva Goode, Helen Harrison, Judy Hartstone, Phyllis Karas, Terry Ann Knopf, Joanna Lennon, Julia Lieblich, Ronnie Londner, Melissa Ludtke, Carol Mann, Carolyn Toll Oppenheim, Caryl Rivers, Mary Rourke, Barbara Saltzman, Ellen Ruppel Shell, Alice Short, Jeannette Smyth.

Thank you, Susan Menchin, for watching so carefully over Sam while I was glued to my word processor.

Thanks, Mom.

And to Fox, Sam, Ethan, and Sarah, thank you.

FOR

Emily Eaton Butterfield, Kate Gilmore Anderson,
Kenneth Neil Levy, and David Charles Laertes Saltzman—
playmates in Heaven.
May their spirits soar.

Contents

Weeping may endure in the night
But joy comes in the morning.

—Psalms 30:6, *Book of Common Prayer*

Foreword

Coming face to face with the Angel of Death rarely brings out the best in anyone. Whether we are confronting our own mortality, whether we are the parents of a dying or murdered child, or whether we are the friends of someone newly bereaved, we feel frightened, angry, and helpless. And sometimes, in our emotional confusion, feeling we need to do something or say something, we do or say the wrong thing. One of the virtues of this book is that, whatever your connection to the child who has died, it will help you to know what to do and say.

In this book, you will meet parents who could not let themselves grieve for fear that it would hurt more than they could bear. And you will meet parents who could not stop grieving for fear that if they ever got over their loss and saw their lives return to normal, they would lose their child again, this time even more permanently. You will meet parents who were determined to redeem their child's death from meaninglessness by creating an award, writing a book, or getting a law passed. If you are a parent who has lost a child, you will meet yourself in this book, in all of your pain, and you will be helped by learning that you are not alone.

When our fourteen-year-old son Aaron died of a congenital ailment, my wife and I joined the local chapter of Compassionate Friends, a network of support groups for bereaved parents. (It has been called "the club with the highest membership dues in the world.") I learned that a support group, when it works, can work wonders.

You feel so alone when your child has died, so singled out by adverse fate, so bereft in a world of happy, intact families. Then you join a support group and realize how many other people like you are out there. I don't have very much in common with the Kennedys, the Rockefellers, or the Bushes, but we have all experienced the heartbreak of the death of a child. As this book testifies, the loss of a child can afflict the high and the low, the famous and the anonymous, the poet and the inarticulate parent.

The support group not only helps you heal. It positions you to help others heal, to say and do what they need because you have been there, and you know. This is what Elizabeth Mehren has done with her grief in writing this book.

After the Darkest Hour answers the most important question a bereaved parent asks: "Will I ever get over it?" And the answer is yes and no. No, you will never be the same person you were before. In the nearly twenty years since our son died, not a day has passed that I haven't thought about him. His life and death define who I am more than any other single event. But yes, you do reach the point where remembering does not overwhelm you as it did in the beginning. You survive to see the day when you can love and laugh and enjoy the sunshine without feeling that you are betraying your child by doing so. You realize that on the contrary, you are living his unlived years for him and with him. We heal, but we remember, and living with the memory is part of the healing.

Rabbi Harold S. Kushner
Natick, Massachusetts

AFTER
THE DARKEST HOUR

———

THE SUN WILL SHINE
AGAIN

Farewell, thou child of my right hand, and joy;
My sin was too much hope of thee, loved boy;
Seven years thou wert lent to me, and I thee pay,
Exacted by thy fate, on the just day.
O, could I lose all father now. For why
Will man lament the state he should envy?
To have so soon 'scaped world's, and flesh's rage,
And, if no other misery, yet age?
Rest in soft peace, and, asked, say here doth lie
Ben Jonson his best piece of poetry.
For whose sake, henceforth, all his vows be such,
As what he loves may never like too much.

—Ben Jonson, *"On My First Son"*

1: At a Loss for Words

What do you say when a child dies?

It's a question our culture labors to avoid.

With bounty ever beckoning, we are ill-equipped to deal with loss of any kind. Loss suggests privation, a notion that makes us shudder, then hurry to change the subject. In business, loss connotes financial devastation; in sports it means defeat. A treasured object that is lost makes us pine to possess it once again. Loss of face, or self-respect, is grounds for mortification. Even a "lost dog" poster nailed to a tree gives us pause. How is that family holding up without dear old Buster, we cannot help but wonder.

But death, the ultimate loss, makes us most uncomfortable of all.

A child's death is loss to the nth degree; it is perdition of the worst persuasion, its limits pushed somewhere out there to the edge of the solar system.

When a child perishes, we are plunged into a deep and chilly well where questions bounce from every wall. We are forced to examine some of our most basic beliefs and assumptions. We must probe our notions about parenthood. We must scrutinize our views about what we understand to be the natural order of life.

Our family knows this all too well, and firsthand. Our precious firstborn child, our daughter Emily, succumbed to a devastating disease, an intestinal infection we could barely pronounce. We had never even heard of necrotizing enterocolitis, and suddenly here it was, killing our child. Along with the stages of grief that we are all told to expect—the shock, denial, anger, guilt, and depression—we found ourselves questioning certain basic tenets we had always taken for granted. Children are supposed to outlive their parents, aren't they? Are you still a mother—I mean, do you still get to wear the label?—even after your child is dead? Do you bury your dreams along with your child?

This kind of reflection can be excruciating. It is physically exhausting and emotionally debilitating. Wondering "why" (which finally is the purpose of all this inquisition) leaves us flattened. A headline above a recent newspaper article about parents who had lost children probably understated the toll this kind of anguish exacts when it declared, "It's the worst pain."

Burying a child stands the world on its head. Everything that we most cherish is inverted, back-to-front, out of synch. We wonder how the world can have the conceit to carry on when our own private universe has been decimated. We marvel that people can still play golf, go to the grocery story, paint their houses, polish their nails. The daily minutiae of life seem unimaginably trivial in the shadow of youthful death.

And words?

Well, most of us are at a loss for words.

> *Whom the Gods love dies young.*
>
> —Menander, *"The Double Deceiver"*

SUSY CLEMENS

He wrote so much, and most of us have read so much of what he wrote. We begin, as children, with *Tom Sawyer,* or maybe *Huckleberry Finn.* Growing up in northern California, I was raised on "The Celebrated Jumping Frog of Calaveras County," set not far from where my father's family settled at the time of the Gold Rush.

So prolific was he as a writer that it's hard to imagine this giant of American letters, Mr. Samuel Clemens— Mark Twain—struggling to express himself. Since he was a humorist, wry and ironic, it's hard to picture him dour. Yet Clemens was a father, too, and he doted on his bright, sunny daughter Susy. The news that meningitis had claimed her life at twenty-four rendered him speechless. Clemens was standing in his dining room when the cable informing him of Susy's death reached him. Later he would recall that he was unable at that moment to respond. He could find no words.

His daughter's formal name was Olivia Susan. Clemens adored her. Eight full years after her death, Clemens was still groping to articulate his grief. What he said, finally, was that trying to put his loss into words was futile. To do so, he wrote, "would bankrupt the vocabulary of all the languages."

When nearly ten years had passed since Susy's death, Clemens continued to grapple with his fatherly grief. "It is one of the mysteries of our nature," he wrote, "that a man, all unprepared, can receive a thunder-stroke like that and live."

In his 1924 *Autobiography*, Clemens remained reflective about Susy's death, his grief still unresolved. The following passage reflects the experience of so many parents who find that as devastating as it may be to learn of a child's death, that is only the beginning of a hairpin-curved emotional ride.

"The intellect is stunned by the shock and but gropingly gathers the meaning of the words," Clemens wrote. "The power to realize their full import is mercifully still wanting. The mind has a dim sense of vast loss—that is all. It will take mind and memory months and possibly years to gather the details and thus learn the whole extent of the loss."

OLIVIA SUSAN CLEMENS
1872–1896

After the Darkest Hour

The joys of parents are secret, and so are their griefs and fears:
They cannot utter the one, nor will they utter the other.

—Francis Bacon, *"Of Parents and Children"*

2: The Kindest Words

Yet words are what the world wants to offer. They mean well, these friends and relatives and—occasionally—near-strangers who shower us with what they see as solace in the hours and days and weeks that follow the death of a child. Words are a cushion, or at least that is what many people seem firmly to believe; they shield us somehow from our sadness.

And sometimes they are right, of course. The right word at the right time is a true gift. It's a balm that can make the recipient and the giver feel better.

Unfortunately, the formula is not always so simple.

There are days as a grieving parent when you feel that you are standing in the midst of a verbal torrent. If you were a cartoonist, you could sketch the phrases falling out of the sky, the humble clichés of death. Most are harmless. Virtually all are well-intentioned. "Oh what a shame," they say. (And they are absolutely correct.) "Time heals all wounds." (Well, maybe—but for sure it will take a lifetime to find out.) But still, some sting. "At least you had him/her as long as you did."

(My child, you want to respond, was not a library book.) The worst of all, bar none, is the maxim we seem to hear the most—it makes me cringe even to write it here: "I know how you feel." (My advice on this one is to walk away, as quickly and as politely as possible. How could anyone presume to know how another human being feels?) Another of my personal unfavorites, this one reserved for parents who have lost young children: "There, there, you'll have another one." My husband and I heard that one a lot. It never got easier, for all the repetition.

Or there was the colleague who thumped me on my back three months after my daughter died. "All healed?" she asked cheerily, a giant fearsomely friendly grin on her face. I could not bring myself to smile back. But as politely as I could, I told her I doubted that I would ever be "all healed."

There is no umbrella to protect us from this kindhearted outpouring, nor should there be. The second, third, or forty-fourth time that you hear "I know just how you feel," you might want to square off and challenge the person who says it to you. But for what purpose? Usually, it is benign ignorance that prompts even the most awkward attempts at sympathy. Family and friends have grieving of their own to do. By reaching out to you, they may be sorting through their own sadness. By extending an arm, or a word, of support, they may buttress themselves as well. It's a hard, treacherous path, this road we wander in the wake of a child's death. So often it is words that cause us to stumble.

So what do you say when a child dies, when a tiny life leaves the planet far too soon? What words do you offer, knowing that none can ever equal the loss?

You say the words that we as parents most long to hear.
You say, "I'm sorry. And I care."

What the mother sings to the cradle goes all the way down to the coffin.

—Henry Ward Beecher, *"Proverbs from Plymouth Pulpit"*

BENJAMIN ERNEST LINDER

Here is Ben Linder, wearing a giant red clown nose, huge floppy clown shoes, white greasy clown paint, and a grin that might itself replace electric lighting in this Central American country. Ben is a magnet this day in El Cua, Nicaragua. Children follow him as he weaves his unicycle through the town. They can feel his magic, and they want to be a part of it. They are laughing, smiling, skipping. Nothing gives this young mechanical engineer more pleasure than to see the joy in the faces of these boys and girls. "The children are born to be happy," Ben explains to friends and family in Portland, Oregon, borrowing from a Nicaraguan saying that shows how children are treasured, even in a culture wracked by war.

Here is Ben Linder again. Now he is demonstrating the steps that have gone into constructing a hydroelectric plant to serve the people in the rural, mountainous region of Cua-Bocay. Ben has vowed to use his education to improve conditions in a region where, as he once wrote to his sister Miriam, "people historically have had a hard life." Ben is a wiry fellow, perhaps 120 pounds. He has grown a beard here in Nicaragua. It has come in red and curly, and a little bit wild. He is showing off a piece of equipment donated by the government of Sweden. His explanation grows technical. And then, because Ben can laugh at these abstruse mechanical discussions, he adds, "Basically, it looks like a squirrel cage."

One final glimpse of Ben. This is the last time we shall see him—in a wooden casket. He has been shot, murdered by United States–sponsored contra rebels on the morning of April 28, 1987. Bullets disabled him, and then his assassins fired a gun through his head at point-blank range. Ben was twenty-seven years old. He was working without salary in Nicaragua, working to improve the living conditions of these people who, historically, have had a hard life. They are lifting his coffin now, and again, a crowd is following him, thousands of people who are marching to honor him in the town of Matagalpa, where he will be buried. Among the pallbearers is Nicaraguan president Daniel Ortega, who speaks passionately at Ben Linder's funeral. Ben's family is there, too, his mother Elisabeth, his father David, his brother John, his sister Miriam. Amidst the throng we see a grim-faced friend of Ben's, a woman who is holding aloft a hand-printed sign. "They Can Cut the Flowers," it reads, "But They Will Never Stop the Spring."

Struggling to process the monstrous cruelty of his son's death, David Linder recalls, "He was a sweet little kid, trying to do the right thing and not hurt anybody. And he got killed."

At her son's memorial service, Elisabeth Linder remembers

how Ben, a shy and fearful child, harbored a terrible dread of crossing bridges. It seemed so fitting, somehow, that the boy who was afraid to cross bridges grew up to become a symbol of building bridges, between people and between nations. And so, in their grief, the Linders pledge to memorialize their son by undertaking a speaking project, the Ben Linder Peace Tour, that will take them to forty-three states and around the world. They set about raising funds to complete the facility in San José de Bocay that will now and forever be known as "Central Mini-Hidroeléctrica Benjamin Linder," the Benjamin Linder Hydroelectric Plant.

"You start these dreams, about your child, when you first become pregnant," Elisabeth Linder says.

She knows that these dreams go on and on. They never stop. Ever.

BENJAMIN ERNEST LINDER
1960–1987

3: The Family Secret

So often, when a child dies, a family feels compelled to try to bury the sadness along with the child. Officially, anyway, the sorrow becomes a secret. Social pressures conspire to make it less harrowing to avoid the discussion entirely than to face the questions or the judgments—real or imagined—that accompany a child's death. Until very, very recently, many parents labored under the belief that acknowledging a dead child would severely traumatize their living children. Greeting card companies have only lately begun to manufacture sentiments in categories as specific as "loss of son" or "loss of daughter."

So for some parents, a child's death is best stuffed away in a safe spot for hiding, a place that only they can visit.

But can it ever really go away?

This painful conundrum became apparent once again following a recent conversation with my friend Mary. Mary was engaged to be married, and was bubbling over with all the joy and excitement that a bride is entitled to. She and Mark, her fiancé, were enthralled with the process of mutual discovery that comes with planning a wedding.

But amidst the elation, Mary was surprised when, almost

casually, Mark mentioned that he had had a sister who died before he was born. Mary was stunned. What was her name? she wanted to know. Mark shook his head. His parents had never told him; the subject was not something the family dwelled on. How had she died? Mary pressed. Again, Mark was at a loss. She died as a baby. That was all he knew.

The story gnawed at Mary. Boldly, and because she wanted to learn more about the family she was marrying into, she decided to raise the topic of Mark's sister at the next family gathering.

At first Mark's mother looked shocked, as if Mark had revealed a deep and embarrassing confidence that was better left forgotten. But then she softened. Imagine the surprise of Mark and his own sister as their mother told them for the first time that the baby was named Martha, and that Martha succumbed to crib death, right there in their home, before she was a year old.

Mary asked Mark's mother to tell her about Martha. With her adult children mesmerized, she described a beautiful little girl with alabaster skin, curly dark hair, and shiny, sparkly blue eyes. She talked about Martha's little laugh, and how it tinkled, like music. Martha's favorite toy was a stuffed lamb. Her blanket was yellow, crocheted by a favorite aunt. The lamb and the blanket were in a little box in the attic. Martha's lacy bonnet was there, too.

Before long the whole family was in tears. Mary, too, was weeping. But she also felt uncomfortable, embarrassed because she, the outsider, had pried open this long-locked door of anguish. She took Mark's mother aside and tried to apologize for her brashness.

After the Darkest Hour

Mark's mother would have none of Mary's chagrin.

"We should have had this conversation long ago," she said. "But no one ever asked. No one felt like they had permission. I suppose I was afraid to reopen the wound myself." She slipped her arm around her future daughter-in-law. "But hiding it never did make it go away."

Along with the celebratory champagne, weddings must have a way of uncorking these family secrets. Another friend flew off to visit an aging aunt, bringing with him the exciting news that at the age of forty-five, he was about to be married. His aunt, ninety-two, demanded a description of his fiancée.

"Well," he began, "Barbara is—"

But before Alex could go on, his aunt interrupted him. "Barbara?" she said. "Why, Barbara was the name of my little girl. She was three years old when she died." Sixty-four years after the child's death, his aunt launched into a vivid recollection, occasionally punctuated by tears. Alex was dumbfounded. For his entire life he had assumed that his aunt, a fashion designer with an international reputation, was childless. No one had ever said a word to the contrary.

To celebrate the new family they were creating by the act of their marriage, Mark and Mary each read a small speech in honor of their families at their wedding ceremony. Then, together they lit a single white candle and turned to face their guests.

"This is for Martha," Mary said. "Mark's big sister . . ."

Mark picked up where his bride left off.

" . . . Who lives in our hearts," he said. "And who is a part of our family, too."

In our own family we have taken much the same approach.

Though some friends and relatives questioned our judgment, we have chosen to include Emily as a member of our family, even in death. From the time Sam was a baby, we talked warmly and lovingly of Emily. It filled me with joy when his most treasured object became a hand-crocheted afghan given to Emily when she was born. To this day, Sam drags that blanket everywhere. He tells me, in all seriousness, that it will go with him to college, and also on his honeymoon. He named the blanket "Pinkie," and with no hesitation at all, tells people that "Pinkie used to belong to my sister Emily, who is dead." In numbering his brothers and sisters, he talks about Ethan and Sarah—and also about Emily. At two, Sam was helping me plant flowers at Emily's grave on the anniversary of her death.

It seemed entirely natural, and not at all morbid. Emily's life was not a secret. And neither, in our house, is her death.

> *Dear little sufferer once so brisk and gay*
> *By sharp disease we saw thee pine away*
> *Short was thy stay within this land of tears*
> *And few the number of thy fleeting years.*

> —Epitaph from an early American tombstone

PATRICK BOUVIER KENNEDY

Shortly before his fateful trip to Dallas in November of 1963, President John Fitzgerald Kennedy slipped away to Boston. He wanted no one with him when he visited the grave of his baby son Patrick in nearby Brookline. No reporters. No giant entourage. No phalanx of security specialists. But a close friend who persuaded the President to let him come along remembers Kennedy gazing at Patrick's burial spot and remarking, "He seems so alone here."

The loss of their third child deeply affected President and Mrs. Kennedy. The child came early, four weeks ahead of schedule. By the standards of prematurity he was large, four pounds, ten and a half ounces. But respiratory distress syndrome—hyaline membrane disease, as it is often called—set in quickly. The child's tiny lungs were not yet ready for the mighty task of breathing outside the womb. In 1963, the only cure for this widespread affliction was time and the hope that the baby's body would build its own defenses. In the case of Patrick Bouvier Kennedy, the fight for life proved too much. Before his third day of life, he was dead.

Only the immediate family attended the baby's funeral and burial in Hollyhood Cemetery, close to the house in Brookline where President Kennedy was born. Into his son's small white casket, the President placed a gold St. Christopher medal that his wife Jacqueline had given him at the time of their marriage.

Two months later, the President was spending an October weekend in New England. His schedule was packed with fundraisers, with the festivity of the Harvard-Columbia football game thrown in for diversion—and maybe some good old Crimson glad-handing. Toward the end of the first half of the game, the President turned to a friend. "I want to go to Patrick's grave, and I want to go there alone, with nobody from the newspapers following me." At the cemetery, the President lingered over the simple headstone, with only the word "Kennedy" carved on it.

After President Kennedy was killed in Dallas, and buried in Arlington National Cemetery, Mrs. Kennedy quietly reburied the baby in the same location. Father and son are close beside one another, now and forever.

PATRICK BOUVIER KENNEDY
August 7, 1963–August 9, 1963

I resent "They lost a child too"—as though that were the same. It is never the same. Death to you is not death, not obituary notices and quiet and mourning, sermons and elegies and prayers, coffins and graves and wordy platitudes. It is not the most common experience in life—the only certainty. It is not the oldest thing we know. It is not what happened to Caesar and Dante and Milton and Mary Queen of Scots, to the soldiers in all the wars, to the sick in the plagues, to public men yesterday. It never happened before—what happened today to you. It has only happened to your little boy.

—Anne Morrow Lindbergh, *January 27, 1933*

4: "Getting Over It"

Will I ever get over it?

This question torments every parent who has lost a child. It beats on your chest; it keeps you awake at night; it sneaks up and grabs you just when you think you are feeling strong—and when it turns out you are not feeling so strong, after all.

The very notion of "recovering" from a child's death seems to arise because our culture places such emphasis on moral toughness, on "getting on with things." When you are a child and have a skinned knee, you learn that it will quickly heal, and life will go on as if this temporary setback had never taken place. Unfortunately, we seem to have similar expectations about recovering from the death of a loved one. It is a part of life, we reason—correctly. We will swiftly heal, we tell ourselves—not always so correctly.

While the death of a child is not something we can wear on our sleeves, it is something we will carry in our hearts. Always. We just don't "get over it." Nor should we.

My friend Mandy tells me this story about her mother. Mandy is a full twenty years older than I am. She comes from hardy, long-lived stock. Her mother was ninety-eight, and full of beans and opinions, when she finally departed from this earth. At ninety-three, Mandy's mom joined a writers group in her nursing home. She felt rather superior, she smugly told her daughter, to all those upstart seventy-year-olds who were determined to write the great American novel.

Mandy's mother, Alice, stopped the group cold when it was her turn to read aloud from her journals. For what she wrote about was the death, more than sixty-five years earlier, of her two-year-old daughter. The group wept. So did Alice. Her wall of implacability crumbled. A nonagenarian, she had lived through world wars, the Great Depression, the invention of television, the proliferation of plastic, and the rather eerie rise to power of something called the computer. She had lived a full life, traveling and cultivating friends around the world. She had outlived her husband, an unhappy assumption among women of her age group. But not her own daughter.

"I always knew about my sister," Mandy explained as she recounted her mother's confrontation with her emotional legacy. "I knew she was two years old when she died, I knew she had diphtheria. But I never knew the extent of my mother's pain. She always kept that part inside her, I guess."

Until now. Now she was reading from a wheelchair. Now she was describing the little girl with the dark curls and the dark eyes. She was recalling that child's first steps. She was remembering how proud she felt when this little girl, her first-born child, smiled and called her "Mama."

And she was recounting the helplessness she felt when Sarah, her precious baby, fell ill to a disease that would become obsolete by the time her next daughter was a toddler. For Sarah, there was no reprieve.

Her mother's candor was what shocked Mandy most of all. Her older sister's brief life was part of her own personal history; no one had ever hidden the story of baby Sarah, and Mandy had grown up knowing about the sister who had preceded her.

But the depth of her mother's sadness jolted her. How had she carried such desolation around with her for so many years, a lifetime? How could Alice's anguish come as such a surprise to her own daughter—a woman who raised two girls herself?

"She just never talked about it," Mandy said, shaking her head in amazement. "And I guess because she never talked about it, we never thought to ask her. It was all better left unsaid, I suppose. Or so we thought."

But of course it wasn't.

Alice allowed her daughter to read the essay that had moved her to tears in front of her writers group. The two women wept together and wondered why it had taken so long to share this cry.

"There simply is no greater pain than losing your own child," Alice finally said. "Nothing else compares."

Mandy had never seen her mother so fragile, so vulnerable. Never before had Alice been so forthcoming. Until now, her pain at the loss of her baby had remained purely private.

The honesty of her emotions that day convinced Mandy of the scope of her mother's heartache.

"You think you should get over it," Alice said. "You think you will get over it. But you never do. You never really do."

So now when a newly grieving mother looks at me with those haunted, hurt-filled eyes, and asks, "Will I ever get over it?" I reply, "No." That may sound cold, and usually I try to temper my response with some gentle gesture. But it seems to me that grieving parents spend a great deal of time expecting the impossible of themselves. Expecting to miraculously recover—which of course we all wish our children had been able to do—from a life-changing experience of this magnitude is a mission doomed to failure. You don't "get over it."

But you do go on. You go on as a changed person: strong, because you have withstood the ultimate test that any mortal can confront—and strong, too, because if you are lucky, you will have an angel you can summon in dark, dreary moments.

O, fare ye well my darling girl
Your mother's pleasure and her joy
The treasure of your father's heart,
'Tis hard, my darling girl, 'tis hard to part.

—From the announcement of the
death of Sarah Ann Burditt,
nine years old, *May 12, 1874*

JENNIFER KENNEY FOLSOM

On the fifth anniversary of her daughter's death, June Kenney was taken aback by the fierceness of her emotions. As she does every year on the fifth of September, and as she often does on ordinary days throughout the year, June climbed the hill near her house in Fayston, Vermont, to spend some time at the quiet family plot where Jennifer Kenney Folsom is buried beside her husband Doug and their three-year-old daughter Angie. June was carrying pots of flowers to plant at her daughter's grave. She paused to rub her hand across the stone marker. It had taken June and Don Folsom more than a year after Jenny's death to acknowledge the event with a gravestone. The stone connoted a finality that neither June nor Don felt ready to impose on her death. It was nicer, in some ways, they say even now, when the ashes of their daughter, granddaughter, and son-in-law were buried unmarked on the hill behind the Kenneys' home.

As she stroked the marker, June was amazed by the feelings that suddenly overtook her.

"I was mad! I was furious!" June said. "I just stood there, at the grave, and gave the stone a few solid whacks. All I could say was, 'What a waste. What a waste.'"

After five years, June assumed she had moved far past rage. But her anger followed her back down the hill, to her home. It's a good thing no one came to the door just then, June said, because she probably would have punched them out. "Didn't matter who it was. I was mad at everyone, the whole world."

In her native Vermont, the story of Jennifer Kenney Folsom is so familiar that when June had a stress-induced heart attack three years after her daughter's death, a cardiologist needed only to hear Jenny's name to understand the source of this mother's anguish. Blonde and blue-eyed, Jenny was a hairdresser who bore a striking resemblance to June. Everyone in tiny Fayston, population 846, knew the family, and knew Jenny and her bright, easy smile. Doctors in this rural area told Jenny she must have a particularly virulent form of flu when her persistent listlessness and diarrhea failed to respond to medication. Even the doctors took no note of the painful white sores in Jenny's mouth. Jenny was heterosexual. She was married. She had no history of drug abuse. And this was rural Vermont. City scourges like AIDS were not part of the local topography.

Soon after Jenny gave birth to Angie, her second child, her blood test came back positive for HIV, the virus that causes AIDS. "I thought, 'No way, they got it wrong,'" June remembered. "Not my kid."

To protect themselves from the narrow-mindedness they feared awaited them if they told the truth, the Kenney-Folsom family put out the word that Jenny had leukemia. When Angie was found to be HIV-positive, just after her first birthday, they said wasn't that a coincidence?, the baby had leukemia, too.

But the stress and the secrecy and the storytelling took their toll on the family. After four years of sobriety, Doug Folsom began drinking heavily. When Jennifer finally chose to inform a small circle of friends about the true nature of her illness, Doug "just kind of went into his shell," his mother-in-law recalled. He feared people would judge him. He feared business

After the Darkest Hour

at his auto body shop would dry up. One day, he left a tape-recorded message for Jenny, telling her to "hang tough." Then he climbed into the hammock outside their home and shot himself to death. In a letter to the local newspaper that ran with her husband's obituary, Jenny wrote that Doug "had danced as long as he could."

Privately, Jenny made a vow to live long enough to see her older daughter Nicolette board the bus for her first day of school. She died the day after achieving that goal. Her daughter Angie, by then three years old, followed her mother in death six weeks later.

In the last three months of her life, Jenny blossomed into a public campaigner, promoting AIDS awareness. On her deathbed, she pulled her mother close and made June promise to keep up the work. She did, with such intensity that within a year of Jenny's death, June was named Vermont's Mother of the Year. To this day, June thinks the award belonged rightfully to Jenny. "She woke up an awful lot of people," June said. "Even the old dyed-in-the-wool straitlaced Vermonters."

One point that mother and daughter alike chose to emphasize is that AIDS is a virus, not a value judgment. How Jenny contracted the disease is nobody's business, her mother insists: "What difference does it make?" Years ago, Kenney conceded, she would have offered harsh judgments herself. But after watching AIDS ravage her family, and after joining the only AIDS support group in Vermont (in which June and Jenny were the only nonmale, nonhomosexual members), she concluded that "How someone got AIDS doesn't matter. What matters is that they have the disease and that we deal with them with love."

At ten years old Niki Kenney looks exactly like her mother. Walks like Jenny. Talks like Jenny. Laughs like Jenny. "Sometimes it's like we haven't really lost Jenny, like she's right there, but she's Niki instead," June says.

But the trips to the graveyard remind June and Don Folsom that their daughter is dead—not that they ever actually question that fact. Still, when people ask how many children she has, June always answers six, a figure that includes Jenny. She proudly numbers Angie among her twelve grandchildren as well. Sometimes, when they see Jenny's picture among the other family portraits in the Kenney household, people look puzzled and say, gee, we thought we'd met all your children. "There's one you'd have to go a long way to meet," June tells them.

Niki and June have designed an AIDS quilt panel for Jenny and Angie, but they haven't yet brought themselves to add it to the giant banner honoring AIDS victims. "Too final," June explained. But June has stayed close to the men in Jenny's AIDS support group. "I've gone to every one of the funerals," she said. "It's like I became their mother, too."

With every year without Jenny, the hole in her parents' heart seems to change shape. But the aching and the longing for the daughter they lost never diminish. "It gets different," June said. "But not easier."

The wrath that overcame this sixty-two-year-old mother on the fifth anniversary of Jenny's death was in large part about remorse, June said, about regret for a life cut short.

"We could be doing so much together," June said, and with no further words, you could picture this mother and her daughter laughing together, lunching together, hanging out the way mothers and grown daughters often love to do.

June paused for a moment, as if trying to persuade herself of what she was about to say next. "But," she said, "life goes on." She sounded not thoroughly convinced.

JENNIFER KENNEY FOLSOM
1961–1990

When the day returns, call us up with morning faces and with morning hearts, eager to labor, happy if happiness be our portion, and if the day be marked for sorrow, strong to endure.

—Robert Louis Stevenson, *"Prayer"*

5: The Parable of the Mustard Seed

Gotami was a young woman whose every wish was fulfilled when she gave birth to a son. Her son was barely old enough to run about and play on his own when, suddenly, he died. Gotami was stunned into disbelief. She bundled the boy in blankets and strapped him onto her hip. From house to house she went, calling "Give me medicine for my son!"

The neighbors were puzzled. How could they offer cures for a child who was so obviously dead? Finally, one friend urged her to knock on the door of the nearby monastery. The monk praised Gotami for seeking treatment, and by way of remedy, he gave her an assignment. Go to each house in the city, the monk told Gotami. And from every house where no one has ever died, fetch tiny grains of mustard seed.

In every house, the answer was the same. Here, Gotami was told again and again, someone has died. In one house Gotami was told, no one can count the dead. At the next door, Gotami was also left empty-handed. There would be no mustard seed. Here, once again, someone had died.

At last, in sadness and in resignation, Gotami went to the edge of the city and buried her son. Dear child, she said as she completed this tearful mission, I thought that you alone had been overtaken by death. I was wrong.

With her soul heavy, Gotami trudged back to the monastery. She expected that the monk would fault her for returning with not a single mustard seed. But instead he embraced her, and bestowed high praise. You have faced your grief, he commended. Now, he predicted, you will find release from its numbing bitterness.

Gotami knew that he was right.

Job asked questions about God, but he did not need lessons in theology. He needed sympathy and compassion and the reassurance that he was a good person and a cherished friend.

—Rabbi Harold S. Kushner,
When Bad Things Happen to Good People

MAX WARBURG

Raised in an apartment in the heart of Boston, brown-eyed Max Warburg was as much an outdoor kid as any big city ever produced. Neighbors waved and Max grinned back as he maneuvered the busy streets on his favorite means of

After the Darkest Hour

transportation, his bike. He swam all summer, his brown hair a constant sea of thick, wet waves. In the winter he skied, sharing his smile with the mountains. And whenever he could, he joined his mother Stephanie, his father Jonathan, and his little brother Fred and sailed the ocean blue.

Standing at the helm, Max confidently played the role of captain. He was ten years old. He knew just what boat he would have when he grew up. It would be a sixteen-foot center-board boat called a 420, easy to steer and no end of challenge or fun. Long ago he'd named his dream boat. *Take It to the Max* captured his own name, and also his unwavering belief that on the water, in life, in anything, the sky itself was the only limit.

The following year, when Max was eleven, a rare form of leukemia, a variety seldom seen in children, invaded his body. His physicians pursued an aggressive treatment protocol. When it came time to find a bone marrow donor, Max led the charge. He started a campaign to find marrow matches and the six thousand others who needed these vital cells. He called his drive "Max + 6000." Max called radio and television stations, and soon he was on the air. "You may not help me, but you'll probably help somebody," he'd urge. Donors stepped forward, but no match was found. Then miraculously, with Max's condition worsening daily, the ideal benefactor was located, all the way across the country in Seattle.

The treatment was arduous, painful, and lonely. Worst of all, it was not successful. One day, hooked up to four IV pumps, with tubes spidering out of him, Max looked up at his mother. With the forthrightness of youth, he asked, "Mommy, do you think I'm brave?"

For Stephanie Warburg, that question lingered as Max's lasting legacy. Brave? she pondered in the fog that follows a child's death. Could there ever have been anyone more brave? She would wander down the street with no destination, hoping that if she kept walking, life would return to normal—meaning, of course, that Max would come back. She would run to his room and open his closet, running her hands into his shoes to feel where his brave little feet had been such a short time ago. What was courage anyway, she would think at such moments, if not the sturdy determination of a boy who kept on smiling, right up to the end?

Whenever they talked about Max—whenever they thought about him, for that matter—courage was what Stephanie, Jonathan, and Fred Warburg came back to. It seemed their oldest son was the very embodiment of "brave." And it seemed, now, that they were being challenged to live up to his high standard.

Their musings moved the Warburgs to share Max's grace, optimism, and sunny valor. Max was a sixth-grader when he died, so they organized a program geared to children his own age. Within a year of his death, the Max Warburg Courage Curriculum was introduced into the Boston public schools. Sixth-graders from around the city—4,200 students in twenty-three schools—are encouraged to think about the meaning of courage in their own lives. They watch a video showing Max's friends remembering him. They read stories about the many forms courage can take. Finally, in what is described as a non-traditional writing contest, they write their own stories about courage in their daily lives. The best of these essays are reprinted in a book, published annually.

"It takes a lot of courage to fight in a situation where the odds are against you," wrote one of the winners, Jawara McKintosh of the Frank V. Thompson Middle School. As it happens, Jawara was writing about battling bullies, not leukemia. But Stephanie and Jonathan Warburg know that the words might apply equally to Max, who never lost his grit or his grin. To remember this makes them smile through their tears.

MAX WARBURG
1979–1991

Look, in my life you either laugh or cry, there is nothing in between.

—Elizabeth Glaser, *In the Absence of Angels*

6: Courage

So courage is another word we parents treasure. It's a random concept—in that sense, not unlike death itself—distant and abstract, until you confront the eyes of your own dying child. Then there it is, right in front of you, all the valor of a hundred armies: the spunk, grit, and tenacity of a legion of foot soldiers.

Courage is forgetting yourself and focusing only on the fight. Courage means reaching beyond the limits you thought you had to strive for some greater purpose. In the case of our children, that end is survival. For them, each breath is a victory.

Courage is something we hold sacred in this culture. Our poets praise courage, lauding the heroes of myth and of daily life. We give medals for courage. We cheer the firefighters who display courage in the course of their work, the police officers and the everyday citizens who risk their lives during crises. Emblazoned on our world memory, for example, is the man who stood alone before a line of tanks in Tiananmen Square, courageous enough to face off against the entire Chinese army. The *Challenger* astronauts embodied courage as well. And Hollywood manufactures "heroes" on an hourly basis.

People pay good money to see movies about made-up courage. Even dogs and cats win headlines when they perform with gallantry.

Yet for most of us, courage remains remote and untested. On fate's Top 40 list, it boils down to minor acts of mettle— not crying at the doctor's office when a giant hypodermic needle contacts our arm; facing a personal demon with some semblance of dignity; standing up in righteous protest of personal or cosmic injustice. This is not small stuff. But it pales in the presence of the real thing. What a marvel to see courage firsthand, to witness its strength in your own precious child.

You gaze at your child with awe and amazement. Yes, you think, this is it. This is what courage is all about.

At our daughter's hospital, each baby in the critical care area was awarded a nickname by the nurses on duty. They were cute, sometimes: the Champ, for the kid who was training for an imaginary prizefight; the Chunk, a beachball with legs; the Coquette, who, I swear, would bat long eyelashes at any male who passed near her isolette. Others were less attractive, such as the boy who earned the unfortunate (and unfortunately, accurate) sobriquet of the Fussbudget. Suffice it to say that even with a tube in his mouth, that little guy seemed always to be whining.

While I have seen heads of cabbage that were larger than my own daughter, Emily's tough determination was way out of proportion to her size, from day one. From the beginning, Emily was known by the nurses alternately as the Fighter and as Little Brave One. In turn my husband and I soon thought of her as our Courage Girl. She seemed to laugh at the odds, so stacked against her. She defied the physicians' dire predictions, day after day. She withstood physical affronts. Still, today, I picture that tiny package of courage and I feel proud.

Courage is Joe and Barbara Saltzman's son David, who raced the clock to complete a children's book he began writing and illustrating when he learned he had cancer. The book was designed to help younger children—and adults, too—smile in the face of life-threatening disease. David worked furiously. He finished the text shortly before he died, and left sketches for the last few unfinished illustrations.

Courage is every single kid who has gone back to school bald, following chemotherapy treatments. Courage is the adult daughter of a neighbor of ours, whose lethal breast cancer was diagnosed when she was fifty, and the mother of four. Just before Karen drifted into a prolonged coma, her nurse mentioned idly that her own father hadn't been feeling too well either. When Karen awoke, she rolled her eyes open, saw the nurse among the small crowd beside her bed and inquired, "How's your dad?"

But these inspiring examples do not satisfy as a hug from a real, live person does. On dark, dark days, when ghosts and loneliness are fluttering the curtains, courage may seem an ephemeral beacon. What we want is the child, not an imaginary medal, not an intangible legacy. You can't take courage out and push it around the block in a baby carriage. You can't take it to the mall to shop for back-to-school clothes. You can't order it a kid's meal at McDonald's. You can't pass its picture around at family gatherings or class reunions.

Or can you?

Far from scant consolation, I believe courage really is something we can cling to when we think of the child we have lost.

Close your eyes and you can conjure it up. It's there, a gift from your child, and not one single solitary living soul can take it away from you. Courage is your own quiet, private link. It's honor by association. It connects parent and child forever.

Blessed are they that mourn, for they shall be comforted.

—Matthew 5:4

Edward Baker Lincoln
William Wallace Lincoln

Having chosen a family name for their first son, Robert Todd Lincoln, Mary and Abraham Lincoln honored a friend and political ally, Edward Baker, when they named the child who came along three years later. Eddy Lincoln was a lively, sturdy boy. But at four, he fell ill to diphtheria. His parents kept watch over him, rubbing his chest with balsam and nursing him together for the fifty-two long days of his illness. On the morning of February 1, 1850, Eddy Baker died.

His young mother crumbled in grief and shock. Her tears were unending, and only her husband could coax her to eat. Friends say that from then on, Mary Todd Lincoln was never the same. The humor they had relied on in her character was replaced by fearfulness, and sudden bursts of rage. But just one month after Edward's death, Mary was pregnant again. Her third son, Willie, was born in the Christmas season, on

December 17, 1850. Right from the start, this charming, sunny child seemed to lift the sorrow from his parents' hearts.

Willie and his older brother had full run of the White House. But while Robert was staging war games in the Executive Mansion, young Willie could be found in his mother's writing room. By nature he was soft and studious. He loved the feel of his mother's fine pencils and paper. Like Mary, Willie read passionately. His special fondness was poetry.

Early in 1862, Willie developed a slight chill. Doctors, and his parents, assumed he would recover. But his illness was probably malaria. Fever flamed through him. At five in the afternoon, on February 20, 1862, William Wallace Lincoln died.

The President and his wife were inconsolable. Lincoln pulled inward, saying little. His face was grim, his footsteps leaden. The Civil War was raging, and Lincoln, it was said, saw his son's death as another reflection of the woe besetting the country. So demonstrative was Mary Lincoln in her sadness that on one particularly difficult day, the President led his wife to a window of the White House. He gestured outward, toward a distant building that housed mental patients. "Mother, do you see that large white building on yonder hill?" Lincoln asked his wife. "Try and control your grief, or it will drive you mad and we may have to send you there."

Mary seemed to hold a grudge against the very building her son had died in. As he lay in open coffin in the Green Room, she placed a sprig of laurel on his chest. She never entered the room again. Nor would Mary cross the threshold of the second-floor guest room in the White House where Willie took his final breath.

In time Mary Lincoln did pull herself together. She reported years later that she had done so because she realized how much her husband depended on her. "If I had not felt the spur of necessity urging me to cheer Mr. Lincoln, whose grief was as great as my own, I could never have smiled again," she related.

An avid correspondent, Mary Lincoln was loath to communicate in the days and weeks following Willie's death. Five months passed before she could again put pen to paper. She chose her heaviest bond stationery, bordered in black for mourning. To an old friend in Springfield, Julia Sprigg, she wrote of her "sainted boy" and of her "crushing bereavement." Life had changed immeasurably, she told Mrs. Sprigg.

"Our home is very beautiful, the grounds around us are enchanting, the world still smiles and pays homage, yet the charm is dispelled—everything appears a mockery, the idolised one is not with us, he has fulfilled his mission and we are left desolate."

Then Mary posed a question that plagued her through her own final days, the question that has wracked so many parents who have lost their sons and daughters. "When I think over his short but happy childhood, how much comfort he always was to me," she mused to her "ever and attached" friend, "and how fearfully, I always found my hopes concentrating on so good a boy he was—when I can bring myself to realize that he has indeed passed away, my question to myself is, 'can life be endured?'"

But Mary had a life to lead; she was the President's wife, the First Lady of the United States. Her first public reception following her son's death was an ordeal for her, a dismal affair she

After the Darkest Hour

could scarcely countenance. "Oh, how much we have passed through since last we stood here," she commented while greeting guests in the receiving line. Soon the pressure overwhelmed her. Mary departed long before the reception had ended.

EDWARD BAKER LINCOLN
1846–1850

WILLIAM WALLACE LINCOLN
1850–1862

All that was alive we cannot hold, and all that can become we cannot know. But this, at least, is remembered. This, for now, is said. I feel in my chest Anna's wild heart; I hear those trumpeter swans. Sitting out on the swing, I see the stars through the shimmering leaves. And with a jolt I realize that the fireflies are gone—gone from the air and gone from the earth—though I do not, I will not, forget their light.

—William Loizeaux, *Anna: A Daughter's Life*

7: In the Past

In the museum, in the room filled with Roman artifacts, I found it impossible to move from the small stone container. It stood perhaps sixteen inches high, and less than a yard long. Carved in bas relief on the exterior, a family is weeping. A mother and father sit at either end of a divan, one of those classic, armless couches that we associate with classical Rome. Lying on the divan is a young child, wearing a toga, and dying.

Sixteen hundred years after that sarcophagus was constructed, the tears still seemed to spring forth from the cold, ancient marble. The grief of these parents from early in the third century A.D. remained quite alive. I could imagine their helplessness, watching as their child suffered. I knew their hearts were breaking, even in stone.

I don't know how long I lingered in front of that child's resting spot, but I know I felt the family's sadness.

I feel much the same way when I wander, usually with my dog, through the old colonial cemeteries in our town. Our family lives in New England, in a town founded in 1633. The graveyards are small civic jewels, oases of tranquillity and history. They are calm and park-like—the settings, in their time, of public recreation—not the crowded and massive burial sites that have overtaken many cities today, and not the "out-of-sight, out-of-mind" memorial gardens popularized in the California of my youth. These early American plots offer a sense of dignity, and they provide a distinct and special bridge to the people who populated our country at its founding. I gaze at the stone family markers, the names and dates still plainly visible. So often the children died so young: in infancy, as toddlers, as teenagers. Read the stones carefully and you will find many, many mothers buried alongside their own babies, for death in childbirth was anything but uncommon in those not-so-distant days. Follow the family lines through the grave markers, and you see that the fathers often remarried, only to outlive the new wife and children as well.

Up until the beginning of our own century, death was far more a part of life than it is today. This is not to say that it was any less painful for a parent to bury a child then than now. Think of the mother, Lucelia Patterson, from Greenville, Kentucky, who rejoiced when a child finally made it beyond the treacherous first days of infancy. An older son joined her in celebrating, as she wrote in an 1878 letter to her husband. "Willie is greatly delighted with the new baby," Mrs. Patterson reported. "He says he would not have it die for $500."

Or there was Philo Buel Blinn, writing in 1859 in New Canaan, Connecticut, that "Our little babe, aged six days, died last night. She died just as we began to hope and believe she would live."

I think about my own forebears, who journeyed across this country to settle in the fresh new world of the West. It was the time of the Gold Rush, and as the pioneers traversed the plains and mountains, they had little occasion to mourn their many children who died in transit. The unknown elements posed an unceasing threat, and time was a precious luxury, as urgent as life itself. How, I wonder so often, did those mothers and fathers commit the souls of their sons and daughters to soil they would never again see? How did they live with their own empty arms? What became of the cradles they carried in their wagons?

At that time typhoid alone killed thirty out of every 100,000 Americans, most of them children. The young were also the preponderant victims of the forty out of every 100,000 Americans who succumbed to diphtheria. Four out of five people died before they could be considered elderly, and children accounted for more than half the total number of deaths each year.

Surely death was no less frightening then than it is today. But in the period before modern medicine and public health, death was clearly an element of daily life. No one wanted a son or a daughter to die. But the chance that a child might die young was never far from mind.

One reason that a child's death reverberates so strongly today is that we are ill-prepared for this interruption of what we assume to be the normal, orderly, and correct sequence of life events. Expectations have shifted as life spans have extended, so that when death strikes early today, we are surprised. This is not supposed to happen. Science can conquer and cure disease, or so we insistently believe. Laws can protect us from harm. But unlike so much of modern life, death stands out as an event we cannot control or explain and frequently cannot predict.

In the past in this country, parents who lost children might actually wear the trappings of their grief. They made jewelry out of locks of hair, or wreaths of hair that hung prominently in the parlor. Photographs of dead children were not considered macabre or lugubrious. Sometimes the framed portraits even portrayed the late young person lying in a coffin. For pregnant mothers who had lost other babies in infancy or childbirth, special mourning maternity attire was available. Unlike today, when social pressures encourage us to avoid thoughts of death and dying, citizens a century ago and more lived with daily reminders of mortality that kept death keenly in the minds of the living.

By contrast, I remember the young mother I came to know in the neonatal unit of the hospital where our daughter Emily was treated and died. This mother was herself a study in fortitude, having withstood kidney transplant surgery. Doctors advised her that pregnancy might endanger her health, but she was determined to become a mother. Her twin girls were born more than two months early. The larger girl was a strapping two-and-one-half-pounder, a brute by prematurity standards. But the smaller twin weighed just fifteen ounces at birth. Amazingly, that little girl clung to life for two full days. The parents had the tiny child cremated, and displayed the dainty urn containing her ashes on their coffee table, the focal point in their living room. Grandparents, cousins, sisters, and brother, as well as neighbors and friends, all thought the parents—or, more specifically, the mother—had gone crazy. They urged the mother, who spent most of her days keeping vigil beside her surviving child, to see a psychiatrist. To her credit, the mother stood by her convictions. Anyone who was disturbed by the urn, she said, did not have to look at it. "That's our daughter," she said. "She was a fighter, and we're proud of her."

Such forthrightness might not be right for everyone who loses a child. But for most of us, denial doesn't feel anything close to right either. These are our children, our sons and daughters, and like the parents of the past—like the Roman family whose tears have endured for more than a thousand years—we will miss them and we will love them until our own last moments on earth.

There is no difference in the faces of bereaved mothers.

—Israeli prime minister Yitzhak Rabin,
in a speech on the White House lawn, *1994*

BURGHARDT GOMER DU BOIS

With his powerful, thundering voice and his exquisite gift of language, W.E.B. Du Bois is known as the primary architect of this country's civil rights movement. Long after his death, his visionary book *The Souls of Black Folk* lives on as a bible of consciousness and activism.

Du Bois was a towering figure on America's cultural landscape. But he was also a father who ecstatically celebrated the birth of his first child, a robust, beautiful boy to whom Du Bois and his wife Nina gave the imposing name Burghardt. Two years and one month later, when Burghardt died of diphtheria, Du Bois mourned with doleful eloquence. His essay "The Passing of the First Born" captures the universal force of a father's grief.

Du Bois began: "Then the day ended not, and the night was a dreamless terror, and joy and sleep slipped away. I hear now that Voice at midnight calling me from the dull and dreamless trance, crying 'The Shadow of Death! The Shadow of Death!' Out into the starlight I crept, to rouse the gray physician—the Shadow of Death, the Shadow of Death.

"The hours trembled on; the night listened; the ghastly dawn glided like a tired thing across the lamplight. Then we too alone looked upon the child as he turned toward us with great eyes, and stretched his stringlike hands—the Shadow of Death! And we spoke no words, and turned away.

"He died at eventide, when the sun lay like a brooding sorrow above the western hills, veiling its face; when the winds spoke not, and the trees, the great green trees he loved, stood motionless. I saw his breath beat quicker and quicker, pause, and then his little soul leapt like a star that travels in the night and left a world of darkness in its train. The day changed not; the same tall trees peeped in at the windows, the same green grass glinted in the setting sun. Only in the chamber of death writhed the world's most piteous thing—a childless mother.

" . . . A perfect life was his, all joy and love, with tears to make it brighter—sweet as summer's day beside the Housatonic. The world loved him; the women kissed his curls, the men looked gravely into his wonderful eyes, and the children hovered and fluttered about him. I can see him now, changing like the sky from sparkling laughter to darkening frowns, and then to wonderful thoughtfulness as he watched the world.

" . . . Blithe was the morning of his burial, with bird and song and sweet-smelling flowers. The trees whispered to the grass, but the children sat with hushed faces. And yet it seemed a ghostly, unreal day—the wraith of life."

Once again Du Bois was to put his sadness to paper when he composed Nina's obituary fifty years later. He faced up to the terrible toll their son's death had exacted on Nina, and on their marriage. He voiced the lament of a thousand husbands—and of as many wives—who helplessly witness a transformation in their spouse after a child dies.

"In a sense my wife died too," wrote Du Bois. "Never after that was she quite the same in her attitude toward life and the world."

BURGHARDT GOMER DU BOIS
1897–1899

Hearts live by being wounded.

—Oscar Wilde

8: No Safety in Numbers

After they have said "Hello" or "How do you do?," one of the first questions Americans want to ask each other is, "Oh, and do you have children?"

On the one hand, it's a reasonable inquiry. But in some circumstances, it's invasive. People who are involuntarily childless may not want to recite the reasons that they have no children. Some people who have chosen not to have children feel the same way. Mothers and fathers who have lost their children often find the question equally awkward.

One option is to be polite, and perhaps also self-protective, and to say simply no. But for many of us, that response is unsatisfying. In one cold syllable, that response invalidates your child's existence. If you are direct, and offer a response along the lines of "Yes, but he (or she) is dead," you are told in looks or in words that you are making your questioner feel uncomfortable. Friends or family members gently admonish that after all, that person was only making conversation. No reason to put him, or her, on the spot.

Should you have surviving children, you struggle with the

same dilemma when people ask—as they invariably do—how many children you have. Do you include your deceased child in the tally? Again, if you exclude that child, you feel you are erasing his or her life. But describing yourself as the parent of a dead child requires explanation, and tends to make people who do not know you well uneasy. They'd rather you didn't mention it. They'd like to forget it, if they ever knew about it in the first place, and they'd prefer that you did, too.

It's a tough one. Finally, it seems to me, it comes down to a personal and individual decision. Answer honestly at your own peril, for you are most certainly opening up a can of conversational worms. Avoid a direct response and you may regret it later, for you will feel you have let down the child who is no longer with you. But be prepared for this situation, for it will arise far more often than you would like. It's a math problem you'd like to have removed from your own life exam. For it shows, once and for all, what you've always known about math questions: that there's no real right answer—and that there's no safety in numbers.

Let grief do its work. Tramp every inch of the sorrowful way. Drink every drop of the bitter cup.

—Billy Graham, *Facing Death and the Life Thereafter*

CALVIN COOLIDGE JR.

White House servants shuddered as they recalled the chilling sound of Mary Todd Lincoln's howls of grief, echoing through the corridors of the Executive Mansion.

Grace and Calvin Coolidge were no less moved to despair sixty years later when their son Calvin fell prey to a horrible infection.

Young Calvin and his father had more than their first name in common. The pair had similar builds, and in facial expression Calvin Jr. was a near look-alike to his father. At sixteen the boy also displayed a wit so dry that listeners sometimes failed to notice it. On the very day that his father became President, young Calvin started work in a tobacco field. "If my father was President, I sure wouldn't work in a tobacco field," one of his fellow laborers said. "If my father were your father, you would," Calvin replied.

But Calvin was also young, and redundant as it is to say when the subject is a teenager, headstrong. How many times had his mother admonished him about wearing socks with his tennis shoes? How many times had he ignored her? Even in the 1920s, bare feet in tennies were a macho fashion statement.

Returning from a game of tennis on the White House courts on a warm July day in 1924, Calvin Coolidge Jr. said little about the blister that had formed on his right toe. Why would he? Youth is nothing if not proud, and Calvin knew how his mother would lecture him. Hadn't she told him about wearing socks with his tennis shoes? Yes, she had. So he slipped into a hot bath, applied iodine, and set about ignoring what he was certain was a minor infirmity.

But the infection festered. Young Calvin quickly grew listless. Pain shot through his leg, which grew stiffer by the minute. Within twenty-four hours, his condition was grave. In the years before penicillin and sulfa, this condition all but guaranteed a deadly outcome. He died five days after the blister appeared.

President Coolidge, it will be remembered, was almost chromosomally taciturn. When five words would do, Calvin Coolidge uttered three. But friends said that after his son's death, he was a changed man. In what was an effusive outpouring for such a reserved person, Coolidge often stood at a particular White House window and told whoever happened to be standing nearby, "When I look out that window, I always see my boy playing tennis on that court out there."

It seemed that Coolidge could barely move around the grounds of the White House without colliding with some remembrance of his son. Sadness weighed on him. In his autobiography, Coolidge addressed the terrible toll his son's death had levied on him.

"When he went, the power and the glory of the Presidency went with him," Coolidge wrote. "I do not know why such a price was exacted for occupying the White House."

Grace Coolidge, too, struggled to put her feelings on paper. Lying awake all night on the fifth anniversary of her son's death, Mrs. Coolidge jotted down a poem; later, she modestly insisted that the verse "wrote itself." She sent the rhyme off to the editor of Good Housekeeping magazine, explaining that she often received letters from mothers who had struggled through similar losses. Perhaps her small composition would be of comfort, Mrs. Coolidge wrote.

Summarily, Good Housekeeping published "The Open Door," and sent her a check for $250 for her effort. Mrs. Coolidge held on to the check, and gave it to her surviving son John at the time of his marriage. Buy something useful for your new home, she urged her son. Calvin would have liked that, she told him.

THE OPEN DOOR

You, my son,
Have shown me God.
Your kiss upon my cheek
Has made me feel the gentle touch
Of Him who leads us on.
The memory of your smile, when young,
Reveals His face,
As mellowing years come on apace.
And when you went before,
You left the Gates of Heaven ajar
That I might glimpse,
Approaching from afar,
The glories of His Grace.
Hold, Son, my hand,
Guide me along the path,
That, coming,
I may stumble not,
Nor roam,
Nor fail to show the way
Which leads us—Home.

CALVIN COOLIDGE JR.
1908–1924

God, God, be lenient in her first night there.
The crib she slept in was so near my bed;
Her blue and white blanket was so soft;
Her pillow hollowed so to fit my head.

Teach me that she'll not want small rooms or me
When she has You and Heaven's immensity!

I always left a light out in the hall;
I hoped to make her fearless in the dark.
And yet—she was so small—one little light,
Not in the room, it scarcely mattered. Hark!

No! No! She seldom cried! God, not too far
For her to see, this first night, light a star!

And, in the morning when she first woke up,
I always kissed her on the left cheek where
The dimple was. And, oh, I wet the brush!
It made it easier to curl her hair.

Just—just tomorrow morning, God, I pray,
When she wakes up, do things for her my way!

—Violet Alleyn Storey,
"Prayer for a Very New Angel"

9: Remembering

For a young soul, a poem is a glorious tribute, artful in its simplicity. Children do not require lofty monuments to remember them by. In a parent's heart, a child's memory has its own existence and its own loving resilience. As long as that parent lives, so, in a special, private way, does the child.

Some parents do choose to formalize their remembrances. Some plant trees or flower gardens. Some erect plaques at schools or places of worship. There are those, also, who establish ongoing institutions that bear the names of their sons or daughters. At this point, you're probably thinking, Oh sure, it's fine to set up a scholarship or trust fund if you earn a multimillion-dollar salary or you're someone with inherited wealth. It never hurts, of course, to have a healthy bankroll for such a project. But ordinary, working-stiff moms and dads regularly devise creative ways to remember a child.

Rather than money, the main obstacle is inertia—the hazy mire of lethargy that so often sets in when a child dies. Combing your hair is enough of a challenge on these heavy, endless days. Who needs to think about greater goals at times like this?

James and Nancy Chuda of Los Angeles recall the terrible torpor that followed five-year-old Colette's death from cancer. "I was just trying to survive the tragedy, I was in a fog," Nancy said, using the image that so many parents draw upon at this time. If asked to draw their grief, they would produce pictures of dense and bewildering clouds: a fog that sets in with a fury, that seems impenetrable, that threatens on some days never to lift.

On such a day, when Nancy Chuda would have painted her whole world gray, a friend called and reminded her that Colette's favorite color was green, the color of new leaves in the spring. Sometimes it takes a long time for messages to transform into action, for the fog to part long enough for a parent to see the way out of the haze. Three years after that phone call, Nancy and James Chuda set up the Colette Chuda Environmental Fund. Their own contribution was not vast, but they called on every person they knew to help explore the causes of environmentally generated cancers. Word spread; dollars poured in. People who didn't even know Colette or her parents were worried about these issues and wanted to help. The fund focuses on research and legislative action pertaining to environmental carcinogens, with particular emphasis on how these substances affect children.

On a less cosmic scale, I know one father who took up needlepoint after his daughter died. He fashioned a glorious sampler, the kind his own grandmother might have made a century earlier. His daughter's name and dates of birth and death form the centerpiece. Framed, the sampler hangs above the family's mantel, so that every day, each member of the family looks at it and smiles.

Equally modest is one of my own small attempts to remember Emily. I am a voracious reader, so much so that my husband jokes that I should join a support group for "women who read too much." In my fantasies, my daughter would have shared this passion. She and I would have explored libraries and literature together, as I did with my own parents. So now, when I give the books that I buy compulsively and that I have read to our local library, I include an imprint that reads "Donated by the family of Emily Eaton Butterfield, in her loving memory."

Just as there is no right or wrong way to grieve, there is also no one correct way to remember a child who has perished. The memorials are as different as the children themselves, and often reflect the child's personality or favorite pastime. Obviously a memorial will not bring a child back, which is what we all want, deep in our hearts. But some kind of formal memorial does make the child's memory more vital, and often allows other people to understand better why your loss is so huge.

Here are just a few examples of living memorials established by parents:

• On August 30, 1987, ten-year-old Bradley Russell Frye was fatally shot in the back. A fourteen-year-old had been playing with a gun, shooting it out the second-story bedroom window of his apartment, when Bradley was killed. As a teacher, his mother, Karla Frye-McGill, channeled her grief into developing a gun safety program for children. Using her family's tragedy as the focus, she began her own curriculum in her school in New Mexico. In the first year alone, she visited more than seven hundred New Mexico schoolchildren. Soon Frye-McGill joined a task force to address child safety issues. She persuaded colleagues to fund a firearm injury prevention curriculum, using the facts from real firearm deaths of children as its foundation. Inspired by and dedicated to Bradley, the program is now in place in elementary and middle schools across New Mexico and, Frye-McGill notes, "the concept of the curriculum could be used anywhere in the world."

• Ten-year-old Samantha Smith had something on her mind. "I have been worrying about Russia and the United States getting into nuclear war," she wrote in 1982 to Yuri Andropov, then the leader of what was then the Soviet Union. Samantha's plea for peaceful contact between Americans and Soviets led first to her own youthful venture into world diplomacy, and later to the establishment of the Samantha Smith Center in Hallowell, Maine. After Samantha and her father Arthur were killed in the crash of a small plane in 1985, Jane Smith decided that the finest way to honor her daughter would be to enable other children to follow the path Samantha forged in promoting U.S.-Soviet understanding. With donations from around the world, the Samantha Smith Center ran on an annual budget of about $350,000. The funds allowed Soviet and U.S. children to experience each other's cultures in such nonpolitical settings as summer camps. The breakup of the Soviet Union and the thawing of the Cold War led to a recent reorganization, so that the Samantha Smith Center's current focus emphasizes electronic communication between East and West.

• Singer-guitarist Eric Clapton retreated into seclusion after his four-and-a-half-year-old son Conor plunged to his death from a window of a Manhattan high-rise apartment in 1991. Clapton "went off the edge of the world for a while," he told friends. "I turned to stone . . . I wanted to get away from everybody." Six months after the child's death, Clapton released the song that has become a kind of anthem for parents who have lost children, "Tears in Heaven." In an interview the same year, Clapton said, "I wonder, why me? Why have I survived? I have to look at that as the positive. I have survived these things and therefore I've got some kind of responsibility to remain positively creative and not dwell on the misfortune of it." When I listen to that song today, I weep because I can feel Clapton's pain. But I also feel certain that Clapton is singing not only of Conor, but also of Emily, and of every other child who has died too young.

• David Saltzman was a talented artist, illustrator, and storyteller who won a campus-wide following with his cartoon strips in the Yale University daily newspaper. Hodgkin's disease claimed David eleven days before his twenty-third birthday, just before he could complete the children's book he worked on feverishly between the time of his diagnosis and his death. His parents, Joe and Barbara Saltzman of Palos Verdes Estates, California, realized that publishing *The Jester Has Lost His Jingle* would give life to David's talent and to the sunny optimism and passion for laughter that are encapsulated in one of the Jester's own sayings: "Whenever I feel like crying, I smile hard instead! I turn my sadness upside down, and stand it on its head!" They found an artist who could complete the final sketches David left for the book, which is aimed at children suffering from terrible illnesses. The book had barely rolled off the printing presses before the Saltzmans were besieged with demand. The book has been a huge hit, and it is David's spirit that guided it.

• Ruth and Sandy Levy tried to retire from the clothing business after their thirty-four-year-old son Kenneth died of AIDS on Christmas Day in 1990. Ruth leapt into activism, coordinating fund-raising efforts for AIDS programs in the southern New Jersey–Philadelphia area. She began writing letters of support to every parent she heard or read of who lost a child to AIDS. Feeling there was still more work to do, she decided that "in Ken's memory, and in his honor," she would reopen the dress shop she and her husband had operated for thirty years. In its new incarnation, the store became "Friends in Deed," a thrift shop that donates all its proceeds to the local AIDS coalition. A photograph of Ken smiles down from the wall. Ruth is certain that Ken knows about the project and that he is happy about it as well.

• During the eighteen months that it took to convict his daughter's murderer, Sam Knott and his family put their lives on hold. Sam, a stockbroker, worked only sporadically. His wife Joyce took a leave from her job as a hospital nutritionist. Children Cindy and John took time off from school. Elder daughter Cheryl curbed her wanderlust and stayed close to home in El Cajon, California. When former California Highway Patrol officer Craig Peyer was found guilty of slaying Cara Knott, a twenty-year-old college student, two nights after

Christmas in 1986, Sam and his family went to work. Sam lobbied to improve the safety of freeway exits and succeeded in having the unsafe, dead-end exit where Cara was killed closed entirely. He convinced county officials to stop the routine release of autopsy reports in homicide cases. He pestered federal agencies into providing funds for research on DNA testing in sexual assault cases. He drafted a plan to establish a satellite-based central tracking system for law enforcement vehicles. He did it all for Cara, vowing, "We are going to change the system, so maybe this will never happen again."

• After twenty-five-year-old Kevin Wheel was shot to death in a random act of urban violence in 1991—he had stopped at a Southern California stoplight when gang members launched a shoot-out in the car next to his—his mother Teresa suffered from ulcers, anxiety attacks, dizziness, and suicidal feelings. But soon Teresa began to get angry. She stormed into gang strongholds in search of her son's killers, who have never been identified. She lectured gang members at a local juvenile facility, telling them firsthand what violence really means. Law enforcement officials praise Teresa, saying her one-woman crusade is making a difference by humanizing crimes that too often are dismissed.

• *Paula*, named for the daughter who died in 1992 of a rare metabolic disorder, is Chilean novelist Isabel Allende's first work of nonfiction. Many critics have judged the memoir her finest book ever. "In this year of torment," Allende writes as she bids farewell to her child, "I had gradually been letting go:

After the Darkest Hour

First I said goodbye to Paula's intelligence, then to her vitality and her company, now, finally, I had to part with her body. I had lost everything, and my daughter was leaving me, but the one essential thing remained: love. In the end, all I have left is the love I give her."

• My son and I visited a school in Washington, D.C. In the lobby, the first thing that greeted us was a large, colorful papier-mâché sculpture. From the inscription we learned it had been made by a group of classmates in memory of a boy who died several years earlier. The boy's parents provided the idea and paid for the materials, then called on their son's friends rather than commissioning some famous sculptor. What we liked about that life-size figure was its ebullience. It was impossible to walk through the lobby without looking at the sculptural boy, and when you did, you wanted to wave at him, or maybe to sneak out and get into mischief with him. The boy's grin was infectious. You saw him and you felt yourself beaming. You felt good for the rest of the day. You were smiling. Best of all, he was smiling right back.

Before you lose your children, you can talk about it—as a possibility, I mean. You can imagine it, like I did. . . . But when the thing that you had only imagined actually happens, you quickly discover that you can barely speak of it. Your story is jumbled and mumbled, out of sync and unfocused. At least that's how it has been for me.

—Russell Banks, *The Sweet Hereafter*

Vietnam

I doubt if any American adult can visit the Vietnam War Memorial in Washington, D.C., without feeling engulfed by emotion. Whether or not we personally know anyone who died in that war, many of us lived through it. The whole country felt its wounds. I am always struck by the variety of age groups who make pilgrimages to this splendid memorial site. Many are mere schoolchildren, for whom Vietnam is a distant point on the globe. Yet they feel the pull and the power of this place, too. Others are parents, returning again and again to view a son's name. For them, the memorial has a sacred quality, as it should.

For me, the Wall is a magnet. Each time I visit the capital, I simply have to make a trek to the stark granite slab that slices through the earth. I read the names. And I weep. I rub my hands across the carved letters, hoping that some of the courage will reach me by heavenly osmosis. And then I linger over the letters, the correspondence and the remembrances. And I weep still more. These are the messages from mothers and fathers to the sons they lost in battle. Some are propped up on little cardboard platforms. Others are crumpled from rain and teardrops. Some are taped near a young man's name. Sometimes there are small teddy bears attached, or plastic roses. Sometimes there are photographs, invariably of a strapping man-in-the-making.

It is possible that these missives resonate differently for those who have lost children of their own. But then again, maybe not.

Here is Eleanor Wimbish, writing to her son William R. Stocks, killed when his Army helicopter crashed. He was twenty-one years old.

If I could just have the return of one day,
I wonder which day I would pick?
Would it be the one where they said, "it's a boy,"
Or the one where you took your first step?
Or the day that you first played a Little League game,
Or the day that you alone rode your bike?
Or the day that you laughed as you so happily said,
"Got my license, Mom, now can I drive?"

Now I'll not open the door and hear you call out,
"Mom, I'm home, so what time do we eat?"
But I know that God blessed me when He loaned
    you to me,
My Billy, for twenty-one years.
So never again will my arms hold you tight,
For you've gone to your home in the sky.
So until God calls me to be with you there,
In my heart you'll be ever alive.

WILLIAM R. STOCKS
Sergeant, Headquarters and Headquarters Company,
1st Battalion, 6th Infantry, 23rd Infantry Division
(Americal)
May 9, 1947–February 13, 1969

> *A rift in the clouds in a gray day threw a shaft of sunlight upon*
> *her coffin as her nervous, energetic little body sank to its last*
> *sleep. But the soul of her, the glowing, gorgeous, fervent soul of*
> *her, surely was flaming in eager joy upon some other dawn.*
>
> —William Allen White, *"Mary White"*

10: Birthdays in Heaven

"Mommy," my son asked when he was about three years old, "does Emily have birthday parties in Heaven?"

I responded without a moment's thought.

"Of course," I told Sam. Just as quickly I was describing the pin-the-tail-on-the-donkey games that children play in Heaven, the musical chairs games, the leapfrog contests, and the sack races where children jump from cloud to cloud. (That summer Sam had had his first sack race, using old pillowcases, with five other children on our front lawn. He lost, to his friend Cleo, but the game was a huge success.) I told him about the birthday cakes, and how Emily was especially fond of pink frosting. I mentioned that birthday candles have a special twinkle in Heaven, and that sometimes, when you look up at the sky and a star seems to disappear, it is probably a celestial birthday candle being blown out.

I said all this with a perfectly straight face. Sam, in turn, accepted it as God's own gospel truth. It never occurred to either of us that there was anything strange about discussing heavenly table linens or party games. More significantly, we saw nothing out of the ordinary about the notion that children might keep right on growing after they leave the earth. As I write this, looking over my shoulder to make sure that the folks with little white straitjackets haven't come to take me away forever, I feel absolutely certain that my daughter has done well in her first- and second-grade classes up there in the big elementary school in the sky. Never mind that she died when she was two months old. I can picture her clearly.

Her hair is a mass of gingery curls, and she has bright blue eyes, almost turquoise. She is raising her hand and she is asking questions. She writes in big, block print. Most days she is cooperative and inquisitive. But some days she sends the teacher right over the edge, a family trait. Intellectually I know that all of this is impossible. She was far too young to talk when she died. But this is not the intellect speaking. This is the visceral truth, and it's far more trustworthy than the intellect.

Parents of children who have died when they are very young seem united in this knowledge. "Oh, she's twelve years old now," they'll tell you, referring to a daughter who died nine years ago at age three. But somewhere around late adolescence or early in adulthood, the line seems to shift. These parents think of their sons and daughters as eighteen, or twenty-one, or thirty-three—even as forty or older—forever. "He was my oldest," a plump, gray-haired grandmother told me as she pulled out a faded picture of a handsome college sophomore who died many years before. "Now he's my youngest."

But while birthday celebrations in Heaven may be festive—of that I have absolutely no doubt—on earth it is often harder to share the revelry. I dreaded the arrival of Emily's first birthday. It filled me with terror. How could I observe the day this child, my first, entered the world without falling completely to pieces? Yet how could I not observe it? I consulted with other parents who confessed that birthdays and anniversaries were often agonizing. And the worst thing is, so many of them said, with dead children there are always birthdays and anniversaries looming on the calendar. There's the anniversary of the child's birth—*and* the anniversary of his or her death. There's the day the child was taken ill, or injured, or killed. There's the day the child first smiled—or walked or talked, whatever. With the child gone, these occasions take on new dimensions.

In the end, my fear of Emily's birthday turned out to be far worse than the event itself. Yes, I felt empty and sad. Yes, I missed her with a nearly burning sensation. Yes, I moved with a heaviness far greater than my body weight. On Emily's first birthday, my husband and I spent a great deal of time sitting close to one another, saying very little. We took an especially long walk, and we held hands very tight. We visited Emily's grave. We talked to her. It was too cold to plant the flowers we brought with us. The ground in New England is often still frozen even in late March. So we left the flowers for her, hoping that she knew they were pink, and that the petals would scatter in the early spring wind.

We also gave in to every strange emotion. After consulting

various experts about the death of children, I learned that the real experts were the parents who had themselves lost children. Talking to many of them, I realized that the rules about marking a birthday or anniversary, or not marking it, were ours to make up as we went along. We didn't have to apologize or explain to anyone. One mother told me she takes her whole family out to her son's grave site on the two difficult days. They have a picnic. On the anniversary of the boy's birth, they leave a white rose at his grave marker. On the anniversary of his death, they leave him a red rose.

On Emily's first birthday we decided to face our fears straight on. I am a big believer in birthday celebrations—banners, crepe paper, balloons, silly hats, the works. So we held a birthday party for Emily—just me and my husband, since Sam was yet to join our family. We bought her a card, with a picture of a little girl dressed up like a bunny—her totem animal, I am convinced. I baked a cake and frosted it. We put her silver-framed picture on the dining room table and sang "Happy Birthday" to a child who never heard those words in life.

People who have not lost children—even some members of my own family—consider this a ghoulish practice. They are adherents of the "get-on-with-it" school of thought, which we know to be a flawed theory invented by people who cannot themselves imagine the impact of their own child's death. For us, the birthday ritual has become a treasured family tradition. It's a festive moment, an occasion to remember this little girl who brought us such joy and taught us such lessons. Sam now joins in when we light the candles and sing the birthday song. And I always make sure the frosting is pink. Emily's favorite color, I'm sure.

After the Darkest Hour

My breath
    died
        . . . with yours!
My heart
    stopped
        . . . with yours!
My life
    ended
        with yours!
        Nothing is left to me!
        except the Love
            you brought,
    . . . Always, always,
    . . . I shall have
        your love!

    —Joan Walsh Anglund,
    in memory of Todd Emerson
    Anglund, 1954–1992

Christian Gabriel Horchler

Three months after her two-month-old son Christian succumbed to sudden infant death syndrome in May 1991, Joani
Nelson-Horchler had a vivid dream. She felt her baby's warm
skin close against her own. She smelled his hair and saw his
smile. Then he slowly dissolved before her eyes and became
Julianna, his three-year-old sister. Joani was certain Christian
was telling her she had to go on for his sisters.

Soon afterward, another mother of a boy who died of SIDS called Joani to tell her of her own dream. This time, Christian and three other babies who had died of SIDS were spirits who had grown older since they died—to about ages two and five. Christian, the youngest, was dressed in a baseball suit and cap, but was sitting the game out on a log. When asked why he wasn't playing baseball, he replied, "I can't go out and play until my mother does." That was when Joani realized it was time to get back to the game of life. Now she has edited and published a coping book, *The SIDS Survival Guide*, volunteers with several SIDS parent support groups, and has started a nonprofit association, SIDS Educational Services, to inform and comfort SIDS parents and professionals.

Joani is a writer herself. Since this is her story about how her family coped after Christian's death, I'll let her tell it in her own words.

"On what would have been the first birthday of our only son and my daughters' only brother, my husband, three daughters, and I stayed at a friend's cabin in the mountains. We wrote little notes to our baby, stuffed them into helium balloons, and let them rise into the sky. We cheered as those that got stuck on tree branches freed themselves and then danced up through the clouds.

"The friend who lent us her cabin helped us commemorate our son's birth in a special way that we will always remember. Similarly, we'll never forget the kindness of the many neighbors in our close-knit community of Cheverly, Maryland, who organized to bring us nutritious meals each night for three weeks after the sudden death of our child put us under extreme, almost intolerable stress. One family lent us their beachhouse; another baby-sat for a weekend so Gabe and I could get away as a couple. My mother and my sister had me call them collect at any time of the night or day when I needed to talk.

"In fact, the most helpful things friends and relatives do for us is simply to let us talk about our grief. Some people are fearful of 'reminding' survivors of the child who has died, but they shouldn't be—the baby is always in our minds, anyway, and it helps us to vent our feelings. A few friends never once mentioned Christian, and that hurt more than anything they could have said.

"However, don't tell the parent of a child who has died that 'calm seas do not a sailor make' or otherwise imply that whatever good will come out of the death is worth losing the child. Every SIDS parent to whom I've talked would gladly trade any benefit that has come out of the death—such as increased compassion for others—for just one smile from the lost baby. It annoys many of us when people tell us we'll be better people because of all the sorrows we're going through. While we must grasp for any small blessings we can salvage, we'd all rather be our rotten old selves and have our babies back. Besides, it's not like we were ax murderers to begin with!

"Gabe and I and the kids all had trouble concentrating and doing routine tasks for months after Christian's death. Our hearts still feel huge, heavy, and knotted. We had trouble sleeping even a year after his death, but didn't take any medications since about a week after Christian's death because we hoped to conceive another baby and didn't want to take any health risks. I had a miscarriage eight months after we lost Christian which I attribute to the extreme stress of grieving. It took me a year after the miscarriage to conceive again.

"Many people believe that a bereaved parent should be 'back to normal' within a few weeks or months. But psychologists say it's really a lifetime process as parents and siblings continue to face anniversaries and other reminders. Gabe had already planned what schools his son would attend; what chores his son would help him with. So many of our hopes, dreams, and fantasies died with him. His death violated our expectations about the natural order of life, in which he was supposed to bury us, not the other way around. Surviving the agony of selecting the tiny casket and greeting the hundreds of people who attended the funeral turned out to be the easiest parts.

"What continues to be the hardest is waking up after fitful sleeps to the tough reality that we no longer have our precious child to breastfeed or play with. We lost our chance to watch Christian grow, become an integral part of our family, and achieve his potential. With every step, we imagine how life would be if he were still here. Ilona, our ten-year-old, still occasionally writes in a special diary to Christian, always signing off, 'I'll always remember you and I'll always love you.' When Gabrielle was eight, she asked why God kidnapped our baby. At three, Julianna observed that 'big people don't die—only babies die.'

"Our children have been our best doctors. When I wanted only to lie on the sofa and cry, they'd come over and tell me they loved me and drag me off to the swimming pool. I feel so badly for parents of SIDS victims who don't have other children to comfort them.

"This experience won't make me a saint; God knows I'm far too ornery for that. I do hope and pray that one day we will know how life's puzzle pieces fit together and that this tragedy's higher purpose will be revealed. But even if this life is all there is, and even if I never get to be with my son again, I still feel blessed, honored, and happy that I was the lucky person who got to be Christian's mother during his short time on this earth."

CHRISTIAN GABRIEL HORCHLER
March 1991–May 1991

Born of the sun, they traveled a short while toward the sun and left the vivid air signed with their honor.

—Stephen Spender

11: Telling Time

Pardon me, do you have the time?

Ask a person on the street—I almost said a "normal" person, because that is how we sometimes think of ourselves: we, who have lost our own children, as contrasted with "normal" people, the rest of the world—and you will get one kind of answer. Most likely you will get a glimpse at the wrist, and in this world of digital exactness, you will get the hour, the minute, and maybe the second as well. "One forty-two and twenty seconds, August the twenty-first." This is what most people, normal people, mean when they talk about telling time.

But when you lose a child, a giant tectonic shift takes place. If you think of it in terms of chronometry, it is as if all your inner clocks are reset. Chronologically, your interior calendar is wiped clean, but for one key date. There's a new kind of before and after in your life: There's before your child died, and there's after your child died.

What's stunning, what's continually amazing, is that such a vast change can take place with no external indications. When a volcano goes off, the landscape is forever transformed.

When a hurricane sweeps across the coastline, the sand dunes never look the same again. An earthquake announces its presence, and the walls come tumbling down.

Losing a child has much the same effect on a mother or a father. One mom I know put it in terms of water levels. Since her son's death five years ago, she explains, she no longer starts out at the old zero point by which water levels are calibrated. Now she begins at a minus ten. What an uphill swim, she says, it is to read the old humdrum, zero point level. To her that flat point now seems like the height of ecstasy.

My friend Elise remembers standing at the checkout counter in a bookstore, writing a check for a purchase on the fifth anniversary of her daughter's death. The little girl, Lucy, died of a congenital heart defect. The problem was not diagnosed in utero, and even if it had been detected, Elise believes the outcome would have been the same. Lucy was meant to live, Elise is convinced, even if only for nine months.

As she was writing the check, the customer next to her idly asked Elise if she had the date, so she could inscribe her own check. "Five years," Elise answered. "To the day." The woman gave Elise a quizzical look. To her credit, Elise did not apologize, but merely smiled to herself. By way of explanation, she said, "It's an important day for me."

That is one way to look at it—a good, strong, positive way. It may not be an especially happy day. But it is an important day. It's the day your child died, and it's the day your calendar rejiggered.

Since the rest of the world persists in following a more conventional timetable, most of us keep these dates to ourselves. But they're finely etched into our brains, the way we memorize

After the Darkest Hour

other vital statistics, like Social Security numbers or wedding anniversaries. You could shake most of us awake in the middle of a deep sleep and we could tell you how many days, weeks, months, or years have passed.

It's our own secret system of measurement, our own private way of telling time. And it's normal. Perfectly normal.

> *Although the world is full of suffering, it is also full of the overcoming of it.*
>
> —Helen Keller

Stewart Eisenberg

This is a very hard story to tell—not that the death of a child is ever easy—because to this day George and Gabrielle Eisenberg have no idea why their son Stewart took his life in 1984.

Stewart was rakishly handsome, tall, blue-eyed, and dark-haired. He had a delicious sense of humor, exhibited, for example, when his mother hesitated about taking a shortcut through Boston's red light district on the way to a concert one night.

"That's okay, Mom," said Stewart. "Just put your arm through mine and I'll make believe you're my hooker for the evening."

At twenty-three, Stewart had more friends than most much older adults claim in much longer lifetimes. Legions of these young people descended on the Eisenberg household after Stewart put a gun to his head. From all over the country they arrived and arrived and arrived, moving in with sleeping bags and nonstop appetites for the trays full of chicken and casseroles that neighbors brought over. In a scene worthy of Monty Python, Stewart's favorite movie character, they formed a long and blessedly irreverent caravan to the cemetery, led by Stewart's old friend Adam, driving an outrageous bright red jalopy, a silly big boy's toy.

It would be one thing, his parents say, if Stewart had been an antisocial dork with pimples; if he had been on drugs; if he had been despondent or had wrestled with some dark and secret life. But Stewart was, in the traditional sense, a Big Man on Campus, a star in his fraternity and a guy every girl wanted to date. At Syracuse University, Stewart led a campus-wide blood drive. He ran track and graduated with an engineering major. He had a gorgeous girlfriend, a concert violinist pursuing a graduate degree in literature. Not long after graduation, Stewart surprised his parents by bringing his girlfriend for a visit on Nantucket Island. On the ferry back to the mainland, Gabrielle reached into her pocket and found an envelope, a party invitation stuffed with sparkly things.

"Let's throw this into the sea, and we'll be here forever," Gabrielle said.

The next day Stewart kissed his parents goodbye and took his girlfriend to the train. George and Gabrielle never saw him again.

"I don't know how you're handling this," a friend said to Gabrielle as the family mourned their son's death.

"I don't remember being given a choice," Gabrielle replied.

George and Gabrielle are the first to agree that no one "gets over" a child's death. But somehow, you get through it. For George and Gabrielle, a remarkable partnership was unswayed by the worst loss parents can confront. Mystified, distraught, devastated, and riddled by guilt and confusion over their son's death, George and Gabrielle never faltered in their love for one another. They had friends who embraced them unequivocally. They had a daughter, Stewart's older sister Julie. In turn, Julie had a close-knit circle of her own. The glue that bound them all together was laughter: Stewart's, his friends', Julie's, their own. For days after Stewart's death, with the house bulging with his buddies, they all laughed, and they all told Stewart stories. Gabrielle found out why her new Buick wasn't working. It wasn't a lemon, as she kept insisting to the car dealer, it was Stewart the engineer, tinkering under the hood, then putting it all together again so Mom would never find out. Stewart's girlfriend recalled how the two had made love in a cow pasture during a thunderstorm. As the grieving parents were wiping tears from their eyes, not from sadness but from laughter, the family rabbi came by to offer prayers. He saw a houseful of people, howling in hilarity.

"You don't need prayers in this house!" he exclaimed.

A baker's dozen years later, Stewart's legacy of laughter was so strong that when his very pregnant sister Julie had poured herself into a frilly bridesmaid's dress to participate in her best friend's wedding, mother and daughter again dissolved in mirth. Julie was just too funny-looking, so round that she couldn't fit into normal underwear and was reduced to wearing her husband's boxer shorts instead. Julie didn't need to check her reflection in the mirror to know how ridiculous she looked. Instead of appearing dignified and refined, she kept cracking up—hardly the typical demeanor of a bridesmaid. Get a grip, said her mother. Think of something sober and serious so you can walk down that aisle with something resembling a straight face. Think of Stewart, Gabrielle urged.

"Stewart!" said Julie, and she broke into more gales of laughter. "Can you imagine what he'd say if he saw me now?"

But while family and close, close acquaintances were laughing and talking endlessly about this boy who had left too abruptly, there were those who would not talk about Stewart to his parents. That was one of the pains, Gabrielle said: facing people who refused to talk about Stewart and who judged George and Gabrielle with their eyes. A child's death is terrifying to many people under any circumstances. So many avoid or deny it, fearing perhaps that it might be contagious. But suicide is the unmentionable death.

It leaves such questions, so many what-if's, such doubts. Stewart's college roommate had been studying to be a psychologist. The month before Stewart's death, he visited a clinic for suicidal patients. After his friend died, he told the Eisenbergs that he was giving up plans to become a psychologist. If I didn't see this coming, he told Stewart's parents, how can I ever be a good psychologist?

"You're going to do this, and you're going to be good at it," Gabrielle reassured him. "You're going to be very good, because you learned at an early age that not every answer is in the book."

A painter, George Eisenberg is also a veteran of World War II. Aboard a Navy destroyer, where life-and-death situations were a daily diet, he learned to accept life's inevitabilities. This did not make facing his son's death any easier. But it did mean he never questioned its finality.

As a Holocaust survivor, Gabrielle also knew more about death than most people. As a jewelry designer, she also approaches the world with imaginative and open eyes. So, objectively, she was able to agree with the psychologist who told the Eisenbergs that since they loved and respected Stewart, they had to love and respect his decision.

Deep, deep in her heart, Gabrielle knows she will die believing that for her and George, their children are their future. With Stewart's death, she said, "fifty percent of my future was robbed from me and George."

Still, she said, even with only half a future ahead of you, you muddle on.

"Life schlepps you on," she said, "whether you want it to or not."

STEWART EISENBERG
1961–1984

The wonder is I didn't see at once.
I never noticed it from here before.
I must be wonted to it—that's the reason.
The little graveyard where my people are!
So small the window frames the whole of it.
Not so much larger than a bedroom, is it?
There are three stones of slate and one of marble,
Broad-shouldered little slabs there in the sunlight
Of the sidehill. We haven't to mind those.
But I understand: It is not the stones,
But the child's mound—

      —From *"Home Burial,"* by Robert Frost,
         who lost a daughter, Marjorie,
         to septicemia following childbirth,
         and a son, Carol, to suicide

12: The "Normal Pathology of Grief"

One of the many odd and unforgettable experiences that surrounded my daughter's death was my visit to a—how can I word this in a way that is both polite and accurate?—hmm, well, a member of the mental health profession. My husband and my primary care physician were worried. They felt my grief and sadness over Emily's death were out of bounds. They felt I had somehow changed (which I of course had, but it took me—not to mention them—a while to figure this out). They felt I was different (ditto). They decided that it might help if I "talked things over" with someone. In other words, a psychiatrist.

In my grief in those early post-Emily days, I, too, was looking for some magical elixir. I was looking for guidance from someone wise and experienced. I was looking for something more satisfying than the hollow bromides that my well-intentioned friends and family—whose firsthand knowledge of tragedy was blessedly limited—were offering. I also felt very passive, something common, I think, to many of us in this condition. I put on my clothes because, well, gosh, isn't that what you're supposed to do in the morning? I combed my hair because I had always combed my hair, not because I had the least concern about how my hair looked. I did a lot of vacant staring. It was hard to concentrate on much of anything, except the terrible ache that came with losing Emily.

A psychiatrist?, I asked my husband and my doctor. Am I crazy?

Well, not exactly, they rushed to assure me. But . . . well . . . it's just that . . . you see . . . we think it might help if . . . well . . . maybe it might help if you just talked things over with someone.

This is where the story gets interesting. Because after I poured out my heart to this large, overweight, bearded stranger who went to great length to avoid direct eye contact with me, he asked a series of questions to which I was supposed to answer yes or no, much as in a jury trial. But when he asked me

After the Darkest Hour

if I heard "voices that are not there," I was stumped. Well, if I hear them, I mused, how do I know they're not there?

This time he did make eye contact, shooting me an icy glare. "Logically," he said in a voice of clinical dispassion, "you are of course correct."

Since I felt like Alice tumbling down the rabbit hole toward Wonderland—a sensation that many parents have described to me, although not always in those terms—it was strange to hear the concept of logic introduced into the conversation. Since when did logic have one single thing to do with the death of one's child?

After tallying the yes and no answers, the mental health professional came up with the following conclusion: "It is impossible to determine," he intoned, "whether you are suffering from normal grief or from extreme pathological grief."

As if there were one whit of distinction! And as if—if there were—it would make one shred of difference!

Later I learned that "pathological grief" has to do with a "morbid preoccupation" with the dead person, and sometimes is known, less harshly, as "complicated" grief. By either name, this apparently means you are unable to think of anything else, and are honest enough to say so. As I think about it, this characterization is odd, because most mothers I know—myself included—take pride in their preoccupation with the pinnacles and pitfalls of parenthood. We talk about our kids constantly, and think about them even more. Yet seldom is this kind of preoccupation described as pathological.

And so, under the heading of "grieving mother, heal thyself," I left the doctor's office determined to research this conundrum. I decided to stop worrying about what was normal and what was pathological, what was extreme and what was somewhere in between. Grief happens. It's as basic as that.

I went to the library and the bookstore and devoured every book I could find that might enlighten me about this mysterious shroud called grief. (Other parents who have tried this may be able to muster small smiles remembering the surreal experience of standing at an information desk and asking for books about dead children. "Oh yes, right over there, aisle nine . . .")

Here is some of the information and terminology I learned in the process:

• For fear of "being judged insane," as one book put it, most mothers choose not to voice what turns out to be the "very powerful"—and also very normal—urge to steal another mother's child.

• It is also not uncommon to feel bitterness or a sense of injustice when one loses a child. So if you find yourself thinking, Why me?, Why my child?, Why our family?, you are in good company.

• Some parents describe "an irrational sense of self-blame" following the death of a child. I never was able to figure out what a rational sense of self-blame might be. But I do know that many of us blame ourselves. We replay the what-if's of our child's life and death a thousand times a day. Almost always, self-blame is misplaced.

• Grief over the loss of a child lasts longer than any other kind. It heals more slowly and causes the most monumental disruption for those who survive. This is because a child is part of what psychologists call our internal psychological structure—meaning that in a way part of the parent dies, too.

• Most experts believe that loss and helplessness are the greatest tests any human can face. A child's death is off the charts in both categories.

• You may be strong, smart, and highly resilient. But nothing can prepare you for the loss of a child.

• One reason the loss feels so enormous is that a child's death violates an implicit generational contract, that our own children will survive us.

• A child's death also challenges the fundamental instinct of parents to protect their child. That is what we are supposed to do, isn't it? To make the world safe? The feeling that we have failed to do so can haunt us, compounding our sadness.

• In an era of medical miracles, we are less culturally conditioned to expect a child's death than in previous generations. On the contrary, the prevailing assumption is that science and technology can and will work wonders.

• Some experts estimate that in the face of a child's death, two years is a reasonable grieving period. Others double that figure. The truth is, it takes as long as it takes—sometimes a whole lifetime. But if you are lucky, the grief will transmute. Even its physical properties will transform. Its weighty

presence abates. The grief becomes gentler—less terrifying—
and sometimes, paradoxically, rather sweet.

> *Sarah is always with me, always twenty and beautiful, always
> saying "C'mon Mom," with her persuasive smile. She works,
> shops, skis, walks with me. I take her portion of whatever choco-
> late or champagne is served, in a way eating for two again. I try
> to honor her life by learning to enjoy mine again, because I think
> she would expect it.*
>
> —Elizabeth Philipps, *whose daughter Sarah was killed
> in the crash of Pan Am Flight 103 over Lockerbie,
> Scotland, December 21, 1988*

John Gunther Jr.

I was in high school the first time I read *Death Be Not Proud*.
It was assigned as part of the American studies curriculum, and
I remember the teacher praising it for its concise style of writing: a protracted essay from the soul. I also remember weeping,
weeping for a child dying at just about the age I was then;
weeping for his father who so eloquently captured this tragedy.

The next time I read *Death Be Not Proud*, soon after the
death of my own child, I wept again. During that period I was
a human waterworks anyway, so that fact is not particularly
surprising. But this time what evoked my tears was not only
the story of journalist John Gunther and his namesake son but

the brief afterword that followed from Frances Gunther, Johnny's mother. If I had read this section of the book the first time around, it had escaped me. This time, it was as if Frances Gunther were speaking directly to me, one mother of a dead child speaking in the language that the mother of another dead child best understands.

"Death always brings one suddenly face to face with life," Mrs. Gunther wrote. "Nothing, not even the birth of one's child, brings one so close to life as his death."

She described the long horror of knowing for fifteen months that her seventeen-year-old son was dying of a brain tumor. Here she was, writing about a teenager, and yet her emotions exactly reflected how I felt each time I left the hospital where my tiny infant daughter lay: "I never kissed him good night without wondering whether I should see him alive in the morning. I greeted him each morning as though he were newly born to me, a re-gift of God. Each day he lived was a blessed day of grace."

A child's unexpected death shatters every confidence we have in the order of the universe. But a prolonged death raises doubts of its own. Again, though our children perished from very different causes, I was struck by how familiar to me Mrs. Gunther's questions were.

"What is the meaning of life? What are the relations between things: life and death? the individual and the family? the family and society? marriage and divorce? the individual and the state? medicine and research? science and politics and religion? man, men and God?"

Still, such cosmic contemplation was not what moved Frances Gunther to tears as she thought about the life and death of her son. Good sailing weather would make her cry, because she knew how much her Johnny would have loved the wind and the sunny day.

"All the things he loved tear at my heart because he is no longer here on earth to enjoy them. All the things he loved! An open fire with a broiling steak, a pancake tossed in the air, fresh nectarines, black-red cherries—the science columns in the papers and magazines, the fascinating new technical developments—the Berkshire music festival coming in over the air, as we lay in the moonlight on our open wide beach, listening—how he loved all these! . . .

" . . . All the simple things, the eating, drinking, sleeping, waking up. We cooked, we experimented with variations on pancakes, stews, steaks. We gardened, we fished, we sailed. We danced, sang, played. We repaired things, electric wire, garden tools, chopped wood, made fires . . .

" . . . All the books we read. All the lovely old children's books and boys' books, and then the older ones. . . . We talked about everything, sense and nonsense. We talked about the news and history, especially American history. . . . And we also played nonsense games, stunts and card tricks . . .

" . . . Today, when I see parents impatient or tired or bored with their children, I wish I could say to them, But they are alive, think of the wonder of that! They may be a care and a burden, but think, they are alive! You can touch them—what a miracle! . . . Your sons and daughters are alive. Think of that—not dead but alive! Exult and sing.

"All parents who have lost a child will feel what I mean. Others, luckily, cannot. But I hope they will embrace them with a little added rapture and a keener awareness of joy.

"I wish we had loved Johnny more when he was alive. Of course we loved Johnny very much. Johnny knew that. Everybody knew it. Loving Johnny more. What does it mean? What can it mean, now?

"Parents all over the earth who lost sons in the war have felt this kind of question, and sought an answer. To me, it means loving life more, being more aware of life, of one's fellow human beings, of the earth.

"It means obliterating, in a curious but real way, the ideas of evil and hate and the enemy, and transmuting them, with the alchemy of suffering, into ideas of clarity and charity.

"It means caring more and more about other people, at home and abroad, all over the earth. It means caring more about God.

"I hope we can love Johnny more and more 'til we too die, and leave behind us, as he did, the love of love, the love of life."

JOHN GUNTHER JR.
1929–1947

"Our Lost Treasure"

I saw my wife pull out the bottom drawer of the old bureau this evening, and I went softly out and wandered up and down until I knew she had shut it up and gone to her sewing. I haven't dared look at them for a year, but I remembered each article. There are two worn shoes, a little hat with part of the brim gone, some stockings, pantaloons, a coat, two or three spools, bits of broken crockery and some toys. Wife, poor thing, goes to that drawer every day of her life and lets her tears fall upon the precious articles; I dare not.

—Anonymous, *1885*

13: Marriage

You would think, after all these centuries of living together and observing our similarities and differences, that it would come as no surprise that men and women often diverge dramatically in the way they mourn a child's death.

Yet most men and women—or, more specifically, most husbands and wives—continue to be amazed by the divergence of their grieving styles. Unfortunately, the reaction often goes beyond mere astonishment. Disappointment sets in, as one partner or the other feels let down. Then, far too frequently, comes anger—an unwelcome houseguest whose presence seems particularly out of place in the raw aftermath of death. Alienation is another common visitor; husbands and wives complain equally that they feel they are living with a stranger or little more than cohabitating. "Shut out" is another term spouses commonly use in describing the painful estrangement that seems often to be a part of the grieving parents' parcel.

The statistics I have seen about divorce after a child's death are scary. Many reports say that one in two marriages will end after a son or daughter dies. Some place the figure higher still. I saw a claim in a serious professional journal indicating that within months of a child's death, ninety percent of couples are in "serious trouble," many of them headed for separation or divorce. In the end, the actual number is as irrelevant as it is ephemeral. Marital discord and divorce are seldom attributable to one single cause, although a particular trauma may well be the final straw that breaks the back of a sagging marriage. When we are talking about the loss of a child, the actual divorce-to-death ratio is less important than the fact that it is way too high.

Contrasting the reality of marital split-ups is the popular mythology that the time surrounding a child's death is when a couple ought to be closest together, that if ever a husband and wife need each other, it's on the occasion of their own child's death.

In theory, of course, this is entirely correct. Closeness between spouses after a child's death should somehow cushion or muffle the loss. It is as if the two of you together should be stronger than either one of you could be alone, the sum of your joint energies greater than the depth of your individual pain.

But there are good, valid reasons why closeness can feel awkward at this time—and all of them have to do with the variety of approaches to grief and mourning. There are also good reasons for a couple to need what is politely known as space: an undefined but well-understood zone where one partner or the other can attend to his or her job of grieving.

It is also possible that while a spouse perhaps "ought" to be the closest and best companion during this period, that role might be filled equally well—possibly even better—by another friend or relative. Again, this is because each partner is grieving according to an individual timetable and coping methodology. Unknowingly, couples can also compound the stress between them by setting up unspoken and unattainable expectations. Deep in their hearts and souls, each partner wants the family restored to its intact state. They want the dead child back: alive and preferably healthy. They want their own hopes and dreams of a robust childhood for their son or daughter returned to them. So at some level, each spouse expects the other to be not only an emotional ballast, but a magician as well. No mortal woman or man can meet this challenge.

As painful as it is to live through marital strain heaped atop the pain of losing a child, it can also be comforting to learn—or at least this was true for me and my husband—that this kind of stress is probably the rule, not the exception. It's always risky to resort to gender stereotypes. But among women, the common lament seems to be that men grieve too neatly, too quickly. They jump back into work to hide their real feelings, many wives complain, as if to pretend that nothing had ever happened. It's all too efficient to be true.

When blame, real or imagined, becomes part of the equation, things get really rocky. This is little wonder. What marriage can stay on course when culpability is part of the picture?

Another recurring refrain that crosses gender lines is the notion that your partner has changed. This charge, of course, turns out to be true. You are not the same, and neither is your spouse. And because the death of your child is a life-changing experience, it is also a marriage-changing experience. Not marriage-ending—or not necessarily, anyway. But marriage-changing, for sure.

Yet good marriages change with time under the best of circumstances. A healthy partnership evolves. This is not to say that a child's death is just another of those learning experiences that stumbles across your doorstep, opening your eyes to some new character trait in the man or woman you love. It's something that will live with you forever, something that will now become an ongoing element in your own marital equation.

This does not mean the hard feelings will vanish overnight, or that angry words brought on by heartache will evaporate into thin air. But the numbness that may be separating you is likely to let up. With luck, you may forgive each other for what was perfectly normal in the first place—that is, experiencing grief in very separate fashions.

> In the rising of the sun and in its going down, we remember them. In the opening of buds and in the rebirth of spring, we remember them. In the rustling of leaves and in the beauty of autumn, we remember them. When we are weary and in need of strength, we remember them. When we have joys we yearn to share, we remember them.
>
> —Roland B. Gittelsohn

Marcus Yates

He was their baby, the youngest of three strong sons, their golden child. His skin was the color of sunbeams, and radiated as brightly. Flaxen curls sprang from his head, glistening so brilliantly you wanted to reach down and touch some of that bright shining magic.

But it was his dimples that people remembered most about five-year-old Marcus Yates, that and his unshakable good cheer. You could lose a whole finger in each of Marcus's cheeks, so deep were those dimples, and at least once a day, that's what Rochelle Yates would do.

"Oh, Mom!" Marcus would chasten, and then cover his face.

There were hugs and whoops and laughter the morning Rochelle and Tony Yates left Marcus and his brothers Tony Jr. and Malcolm at their grandmother's house, then headed off to work themselves. The house at 59th and Springfield, several Philadelphia neighborhoods away from the Yateses' own home, was filled with merriment that day as eleven cousins clambered around a grandma who loved them all as much as life itself. After lunch, as was often their habit, they all trooped off to the penny candy store. It was a block away, filled with video games and sweet treats that made you feel like a millionaire when all you had was a quarter.

On the way home from work, Tony Sr. and Rochelle drove back to Springfield Avenue. They shook their heads when they saw the cluster of police emergency vehicles. On

Philadelphia's rough streets, it was a too-familiar sight. "The situation's getting crazy out there," Tony told his wife; he remembers his exact words. "This has got to stop. I'm guaranteeing they shot somebody's child."

It was Marcus who was shot dead. The bullet pierced his brain, killing him instantly. It left a wound so deep that Tony, the oldest Yates child, could not come close to staunching the blood when he cradled his baby brother's golden head in his arms. Malcolm, the middle boy, was hit, too, though not as seriously. A nephew, Micah, was wounded in the foot.

"What happened was that while they were there, playing games and being as children are, buying this and that, two drug dealers decided they would have an argument over who was taking over the corner," Tony Yates Sr. explained. "There they were in the midst of all these children, and they decided to have a shoot-out. One went to the back of the store, the other to the front. The kids were trapped in the middle. The dealers just fired. I think a total of fourteen rounds were fired."

When the ruckus started, Marcus had been standing at the candy counter, debating which confection to buy. When the shooting started, his brother Tony yelled to him to get down. In the confusion, Marcus ran instead. He died at Tony's feet.

With their baby brother's death, Tony and Malcolm changed overnight. Tony went from being a straight-A student to offering no more than a surly shrug when he brought home failing grades. Malcolm shriveled up. He stayed in his room, refusing to go anywhere without his parents. The legendary happy-go-lucky attitude of the Yates boys vanished. Now they were acting older, talking older. They became cautious, always looking over their shoulders.

After the Darkest Hour

Between Rochelle and Tony Yates Sr., the transformation was equally dramatic. Rochelle, a devout Christian, turned to her faith. She sought bereavement counseling for herself and her sons. Tony Yates Sr. wanted no part of any outside help. "I'm a grown man," he told his wife. "I've served two tours in Vietnam, ten years in the Marine Corps. I should be able to protect my family. I come home, and two of my sons are shot. It made me question what kind of world we live in. My kids are supposed to be able to walk the street. It made me think that there's just no such thing as the wrong place at the wrong time for a child. We are the protectors of those children, and if we don't do it, well then there's no tomorrow."

The rift between husband and wife became so severe that Rochelle consulted a lawyer, who drew up divorce papers. But her heart really wasn't set on ending the marriage. She knew the two boys needed both parents. And she took seriously the marriage vows she had taken in her church, before God.

Besides, to her amazement, she learned she was pregnant. The baby was conceived just a day or two before Marcus was shot.

"I was totally devastated when I found out I was pregnant," Rochelle said. "I said, 'God, how can you do this to me?' I wondered why He would give me another child to take care of when I couldn't even take care of the ones He already gave me. It was a miracle, and I was just furious. I felt I had no control over anything in my life."

Again, husband and wife viewed the same event from very different vantages. "It was a gift," Tony Yates Sr. said of his wife's unexpected pregnancy. "It happened at a time when we were at our worst. It let us understand that with a new baby being born, we still had to live, and life still has to go on."

By the time she was five, Tanisha Yates looked and acted so much like her late brother that sometimes the family called her Marcus-with-pigtails. She talks about Marcus all the time, as if she knew him, and there are nights when she cries herself to sleep because she misses the brother she never met.

Her parents talk about Marcus, too. "He's still a member of our family, I made sure of that," his mother said. Rochelle Yates also recounts stories about her youngest son—about how his life was so filled with joy, and how his death was so horrific and so uncalled for—when she visits other parents who have lost children to urban violence. She scours the newspapers to find those mothers and fathers. She calls to tell them she's been there, too, and that she's there for them now.

"I tell them 'you are going to go through a period when you're going to think you're crazy,' and you can call me anytime," Rochelle said. "Other people will tell you they understand. But unless it has happened to them, they don't. They can't. I give them my phone number and tell them to call me anytime, day or night. If they need me, I'm here."

A year or so after Marcus's death, Rochelle also decided to open their home to other children. The Yateses became foster parents, sometimes to as many as five children at a time in addition to their own three. "They knock on the doors and say, 'Mrs. Yates, we need your help,'" she said. "I say, bring 'em in. Just a little love, a little attention, works wonders."

As a Philadelphia sheriff, Tony Yates Sr. spends as much time as he can talking with high school students, warning them about the dangers of drugs, gangs, and the stray bullets that may cut them down. "They want help. These children want help," he said. "It's not like they're a lost generation."

But there are still days when Tony feels lost himself, when the absence of Marcus creeps up on him, an emotional ambush.

"People feel as though there's a certain amount of time, and then you're supposed to be over it," he said. "The grief is supposed to be gone, and then you're supposed to continue your life as usual. Such is not the case. There's no moment, six months or a year, when you suddenly snap out of it. It just doesn't work like that. It stays with you for the rest of your life."

MARCUS YATES
1983–1988

That his organs live on in someone else is an extension of his life that has made his death somewhat more bearable.

> —Timothy Flanagan, *whose seven-year-old son Mark died when a cafeteria wall collapsed at his New Jersey elementary school in November 1989*

14: Constant Reminders

The reminders are everywhere. Some days, you feel like you are tripping over your own child's memory. Many days you feel you are colliding with a past that you would prefer to avoid.

Take heart. This is not your imagination or some ghoulish demon playing tricks on you. Everywhere you turn, there *are* reminders of the child you lost.

Take a normal, innocuous, everyday activity: You go to the supermarket and what do you hear? Mothers calling out from one aisle to another, trying to locate kids who are busy pillaging the candy or sugared cereal sections. Most likely, at least one of those children has the same name as your own child's. Instinctively, your head turns in the direction of the child who is being summoned. Maybe there is some consolation if he or she is a redhead and yours was a brunette. But still the chill has raced up your spine. Your breath has momentarily taken leave of your body.

Names, hair color, body types, a joyful peal of laughter, a sob. You may spy a toy, a trike, or a stroller that resembles one your own child owned. In a restaurant, you may shudder to see a child with ice cream smeared all over his face. Everyone around you will be laughing. But to you the sight is too reminiscent of how your own child liked to decorate himself with dessert at that age. Or maybe you are cringing because your child never reached that age, never had the fun of turning ice cream into fingerpaint and his face into his artist's canvas.

Total isolation is probably the only way to circumvent these emotional ambushes. But complete withdrawal is impractical and ultimately counterproductive. You would have to turn off your TV forever, never pick up a magazine or newspaper, and probably throw your telephone out the window. Life would be even emptier and bleaker than it is now. And all of these efforts would probably be for naught, anyway. For what reality failed to provide in the way of reminders, your imagination would gladly supply.

Then there is the equally cumbersome steel-plated-armor approach. This entails wrapping yourself tightly in invisible chain mail, the heavy protective garments that medieval knights wore to safeguard themselves in combat. You, too, are trying to shield yourself from wounds as agonizing as any you might meet in a castle courtyard. But in a way this tactic is no different than self-imposed solitary confinement. You are sealing yourself away, trying to ward off blows that never fail to stun you with their pain.

It doesn't work.

Or not for long, anyway.

The world is just too filled with reminders of what you and

your family had, what you lost, and what you might have had. Sooner or later you will probably have the kind of head-on collision with one of these reminders that leaves you flattened—whacked, in a word. And watch out, if you can, because this event is likely to take place in public. If whatever sense of embarrassment you possessed hasn't completely disappeared by now, it will. It's a near-universal experience for grieving parents, and in an odd way, it's kind of liberating when it finally takes place. It's a dam strained past its limits that finally gives way. It's a weight you've been dragging that finally makes you stop. It's an aimless drive to nowhere that suddenly runs out of asphalt. Time to check your road map.

Perversely and insistently, these reminders creep in not only where they are least expected, but also where they are least welcome. Weddings and family celebrations are legendary opportunities for blind-side attacks. Other rituals also open themselves to stealth-assault memories. Graduations are notorious. When a kind of foster daughter of ours—a young woman from mainland China who became an ex-officio member of our family—graduated from Wellesley two years after Emily died, I sat in the audience, weeping without stop. I sobbed and bawled, oblivious to the mascara river running down my cheeks. It was a glorious sunshiny day, a day of hope and attainment. Collectively and individually, the graduating class held so much promise. Parents were cheering, clapping, thunderously applauding their daughters. And there I was, crying helplessly because my daughter would never have this experience. I'd thought I had dealt with all that. But the truth is, you never really deal with all that. It surprises you with its force, this onslaught of dreams and memories.

But was I sorry I had gone to the graduation? Embarrassed because so many people mistook me for a hysterical mother, tearful because (they assumed) her daughter was stepping out into the world? Not at all. I can still get teary, thinking about that day, about how the sunbeams danced through the branches of grand old oak trees, and how all the graduates tossed their caps in the air and hollered in glee. I can still wish my own daughter would wear the very same grin when her mortarboard went sailing through the air. When I think about it that way, it almost makes me smile myself.

That's the funny thing about these reminders. When you're scared of them—as I was, as we all are at some point—they're vampires in your life, stealing up behind you. And you'd better have some garlic on hand or they'll really sink their teeth in.

But when you take their frightening power away, they're like almost any other kind of demon. You face them, you say "well how about that?," and you heave a giant, well-deserved sigh of relief.

The reminders are never going to go away. And in truth, you don't want them to. At their worst, they are terrifying. But at their best, they are memories to help keep our children alive.

Did someone say there would be an end—an end, oh, an end, to love and mourning?
What has been once so interwoven cannot be raveled, nor the grief ungiven.

—May Sarton, *"All Souls"*

Teresa Jane McGovern

The image that just won't leave his brain is that of a waif, lying face-down in the snow, alone, her bare hands frozen solid.

That waif is his daughter, Teresa Jane McGovern. Twelve days before Christmas 1994, Terry collapsed and died of acute alcoholism in Madison, Wisconsin. She was forty-five years old and died not far from the house where her two daughters, Marian and Colleen, lived with their father. Maybe she was on her way to pay the girls a visit. Maybe she just hoped to catch a glimpse of them through the windows of the house where they lived.

Terry's blood alcohol level was more than three times the .10 level of drunkenness allowed under Wisconsin law. She had waged a fierce, frustrating battle with alcohol since her early teenage years, and was first hospitalized for her problem when she was nineteen.

Her father, former Senator George McGovern, ran for President as a Democrat in 1972. He won just one state, Massachusetts, in his crushing defeat by incumbent President Richard Nixon. His was a campaign that championed a growing opposition to U.S. involvement in the Vietnam War. Terry McGovern was a tireless volunteer for her father, leading a barnstorming bus tour called the Grasshoppers Special that featured celebrity speakers like Gloria Steinem, Liz Carpenter, Arthur Schlesinger, and others.

As a longtime U.S. senator from South Dakota, with more than forty years in public life, McGovern traveled, lectured, and observed extensively. His journeys made him a witness to the atrocities of war, poverty, and disease. Scenes from unimaginably dismal Third World living conditions have etched themselves into his mind—but none so sharply as the picture of his daughter, curled up dead in the snow.

"I can't seem to get that image out of my mind," McGovern said, nearly a year after his daughter's death.

Of their four daughters and one son, George and Eleanor McGovern say, Terry was the sweet one—and the fun one. A party just wasn't a party until Terry arrived. She was no joke-ster, not one of those people who use ostentatious humor to get attention, but she was witty and droll, with a special way of spoofing herself. Her easy, offhand comments put people at ease. She was straightforward and honest, and unlike her father, she was deeply spiritual. As she matured, she said she wished her family would start calling her Teresa. But no one could. She was always their Terry.

In his grief, her father has gone back and studied Terry's elementary school report cards from South Dakota, before the family moved east to Washington after he was elected to the Senate. Her early marks were perfect, and teachers' comments described a confident, happy child. But something about the fast-paced life of the Washington suburbs did not suit Terry. She faltered, and began drinking, way too young and way too much. Her father is convinced that Terry's weak-ness for alcohol was "in her chemistry; I believe in the genetic view." But he also suspects that had the family remained in South Dakota, where life was less complicated, she might have withstood it.

In any case Terry was in and out of treatment almost her

After the Darkest Hour

whole life. She tried so hard to beat "the demon," the code phrase she and her father shared for her terrible addiction to alcohol. She relapsed repeatedly, but never once stopped trying. Her longest streak of sobriety lasted seven years, the period when she bore her daughters and launched them into childhood.

Alcoholism is a family disease, which meant that Terry's parents and siblings often joined forces to help Terry battle her demon. There were frequent family arguments about how far to go in assisting her. One school of thought urged the McGoverns to distance themselves from Terry. But her father, for one, never really did. Terry and her disease were his obsessions, particularly after he left the Senate in 1981. He never gave up on Terry, he said. And she never gave up on herself.

Days after their daughter's death, the McGoverns decided they owed it to Terry to talk about her story. Alcoholism is a disease with a powerful stigma attached, McGovern said. "I know what the public attitude is." The family went public, he said, to help break the taboo. "We need to face the fact that this is a disease that affects people high, low, or in the middle. It is not a respecter of brains or money or character. A death from alcoholism is not a disgrace. It's just sad."

Sadder, in fact, than anything George McGovern has ever encountered. "This is just awful," he said. "It's infinitely more traumatic than anything I've ever been through. Nothing that has ever happened to me prepared me for this." And while people around him have universally meant well, McGovern said, no one can really imagine what it's like to lose a child— no matter how old that child was—unless they've been through it themselves.

Some people have tried to console him, pointing out that Terry lived to adulthood, that she had a full life, that she and her father had many rich experiences together. That is exactly what tears him apart. When a grown child dies, it's still your child, he said. You lose all that shared history. Every time you turn around you see a reminder. The McGoverns were in Spain not long ago on what should have been a holiday. But twenty years before, the senator had taken Terry to Spain. Everywhere he went this time, he saw his daughter.

One of the places where Terry did find help was the Tellurian detox center in Madison. The McGovern family purchased a bench in Terry's honor, and put it outside the treatment facility there. Two Black Hills spruce trees stand nearby, and a solid piece of South Dakota granite bears the engraving "Terry McGovern found help here." There is also a small plaque at the spot where Terry died.

And each of her parents wrote letters to Terry and placed them in her coffin. Her father's letter reflects his regret that the family went through such distancing in the last six months of Terry's life. All the alcoholism counselors advised it, but George McGovern is still not sure that was the right course. He wishes he had talked to her more as someone suffering from cancer, or some other such disease. He wishes he had told her over and over and over how much he loved her, and that he knew how hard she was suffering and struggling. He wishes he had helped Terry to have a higher opinion of herself, and he hopes she knows he was her biggest fan. No matter what the experts say, McGovern has come to believe that "you can't be too supportive, too affectionate" when it's your own child.

He and his wife have agreed that the final, most valuable

After the Darkest Hour

memorial to Terry will be increased public understanding of just how virulent a disease alcoholism really is. The two most important things he has learned about alcoholism are number one, it's a disease; number two, love the victim, hate the disease. George McGovern hated the disease. But he loved the victim, his daughter, very, very much.

TERESA JANE MCGOVERN
1949–1994

"You care for my baby?" the brown-eyed girl questioned, weakly. And then—"Why?"

The old woman's voice was eager. "He is like the child of my own heart," she said, ever so slowly, "like the little son that I bore, many a year gone by."

The brown-eyed girl lay back against the warmth and softness of the camel's hair blanket. For a long time she struggled with a thought. "You loved him, your son, so much, that all other babies are dear to you—for his sake. And yet, in your old age, this son has left you—to the charity of strangers?"

The old woman was holding the baby against her breast. The baby was drowsy. She rocked it as she answered. "My son is dead," she said dimly. Just that. "My son is dead."

And they spoke no more that day.

—Margaret E. Sangster, *"The Mother"*

15: Baby Steps

Be kind to yourself.

You've heard that often enough—although you may not understand just what it means, and you may find it difficult to think about doing anything that seems remotely self-indulgent.

But to me, the first small step—the baby step: there, I've said it—comes in giving yourself credit for crossing the hurdles that other people may not even know exist. For a parent who has lost a child, the main hurdle is facing the fact that for other families with children, life continues uninterrupted. For other families, strep throat is a terrible crisis. So is a lost Little League pennant.

The all-important baby step comes when you gingerly tiptoe up to this reality. It comes when you run into your friend at the public library and realize that she is just as uncomfortable to be seen by you with all her children in tow as you are to be seeing this big happy brood. The baby step that is really a giant step comes when you hear someone whose voice sounds exactly like yours turn to the mother and inquire, "So, are you guys playing soccer this fall?" It all feels very disembodied, as if the words were contained in a comic-strip bubble and were spoken by someone other than yourself. Because asking this basic, nonintrusive question is a gigantic milestone for you.

Baby steps are always teetering, and sometimes you falter and fall. This means you may not really listen to the answer about who is or is not playing soccer. It means you may stammer. Or maybe you'll just wave shyly at the mother and children, turning away as you blurt out a meaningless pleasantry: "Nice to see you today," maybe.

But the baby steps build up. Soon you are downright agile. I think it's important to recognize the momentousness of these advances. To the outside world—those who have not been through the loss of a child—these ordinary encounters will not seem like any big deal. But they are, and you should recognize them as such. Celebrate, even privately.

Here's when I knew my own steps were getting stronger. I have a childhood friend who competed with me about everything. Her hair was longer. She was taller. She got better grades (but only in some subjects!). She got braces before I did. She had her braces removed before I did. She had a boyfriend before I did. And so on.

Somehow we managed to remain friends in spite of this constantly combative posture. She of course married before I did. And don't you know she had a daughter first, too—almost exactly one year before Emily was born. When Erika was born I sent her a golden antique child's bracelet and a silly, frilly outfit emblazoned with the insignia of the college Erika's mother and I both attended. But for several years after Emily's death, I was unable to send that child any kind of "girl presents." I mailed book after book: gender-neutral gifts that I rationalized on educational grounds. I couldn't even think about anything pink or ruffly.

Then one year I realized that Erika's birthday was a week away. This meant also that Emily's birthday was coming up, which may be another reason for the trouble I had facing this occasion. But this year, I steeled myself and decided to go for a girl gift. I think I was on automatic pilot as I steered myself toward the little girls' dress section of the department store. I felt I was in completely alien territory, and I knew everyone around me could see that by the awkward way I was behaving. My arm shot out and selected the pale pink, hand-smocked dress I would have chosen for my own daughter at that age. It sounds foolish, but it was an incredibly difficult purchase. As far as the saleswoman was concerned, it was just another transaction. For me it was a big leap—and one that hasn't gotten much easier when I've tried to repeat it.

The point is that the baby step was a big step. No one else

would have known it, and no one else needed to. I crossed a hurdle. And privately, I gave myself a little cheer.

All the advice-mongers tell you to be kind to yourself as you weave your way through the mire of grief. I think that what they may really mean is to give yourself credit for every single baby step.

> *But grief still has to be worked through. It is like walking through water. Sometimes there is an enormous breaker that knocks me down. Sometimes there is a sudden and fierce squall. But I know that many waters cannot quench love, neither can the floods drown it.*
>
> —Madeleine L'Engle, *Two-Part Invention*

MICHAEL DONALD LONDNER

Strong. Ronnie Londner knew that if she had any prayer of making it through her son Michael's death, she would have to be strong. She would have to be strong for her husband Mark. She would have to be strong for Robin and Teddy, Michael's sister and brother. And she would have to be a whole lot stronger for herself.

This conclusion was not without irony, because on an ordinary day, no one would accuse Ronnie Londner of being anything like weak. She is one of those physically diminutive women who immediately invite the description "powerhouse." You can see it in her eyes, the determination that does not let small stuff clutter her vision. When her daughter Robin's first-grade class lost its music teacher, Ronnie became the volunteer replacement. As her children grew, she branched into a career in legal and medical research. She has been a substance abuse counselor, a children's advocate, and an editor and writer specializing in medical information and subjects of interest to families and parents.

Much of her work has focused on what she politely calls "sensitive topics," meaning childhood disabilities. Londner immersed herself in this field after her middle child, Michael, was born in Miami in 1981 at twenty-nine weeks of gestation—eleven weeks premature. Michael swiftly proved himself to be intellectually and emotionally normal. But his beginning was rocky, complicated by a massive intraventricular hemorrhage, or brain bleed. Michael's birth weight was 1,350 grams, or two pounds, fourteen ounces, qualifying him for the neonatological description of a "very low birth weight" baby. Doctors grade the cranial hemorrhages that occur frequently in these tiny babies on a one to four basis, with four being the most severe. Soon after birth, Michael survived a Grade 4 hemorrhage. Further problems associated with the medical treatment for his prematurity ensued. Nevertheless, when they left the hospital, doctors told the Londners there was no reason not to expect a normal life span for Michael.

For a boy with cerebral palsy, another all-too-common "side effect" of prematurity, Michael was remarkably mobile. When nondisabled children his age were toddling, Michael crawled about on his hands, getting anywhere he wanted, and usually just as fast as anyone else could toddle. In the swimming pool, Michael could walk unassisted, no problem. In time he used a walker, and later, crutches. At age three, he was the only physically handicapped kid at his Montessori school.

Journalist, teacher, caregiver, mother, Ronnie displayed a resourceful blend of strength and compassion two years after Michael's birth when she founded a support group for parents and professionals called IVH (for intraventricular hemorrhage) Parents. The organization has members around the world and continues to grow—"unfortunately," Ronnie says.

Named for his grandfather, Michael had sparkly green eyes, straight brown hair, and olive-toned skin as soft as butter melting in the sun. Of Ronnie Londner's three children, Michael resembled her most, and his favorite thing in life was to press his creamy cheek against her own. For any mother, that gesture is a dream moment. You bury your nose in your baby's hair and breathe in that sweet, special smell. Even today Ronnie Londner can close her eyes and the aroma will fill her nostrils.

Eight years into Michael's life, the routine at the Londner house was disarmingly normal. Sometimes he fought with his sister and brother—they were three normal kids, remember?—but Michael never held a grudge. He wore a huge happy face whenever he brought home a spelling test with "100%" marked on it. He'd boast to his papa, who replied with pride and playfulness, poking his middle child in the belly. That made Mikey laugh so hard he toppled right over. Mikey loved to travel in the family van. He grew so relaxed he sometimes fell asleep. When the engine was shut off, he'd wake abruptly, shouting at his parents to keep driving so he could go back to sleep.

After the Darkest Hour

Parents of very premature children and of children who have endured treacherous beginnings seldom stop worrying entirely. With its roller-coaster twists and parabolic highs and lows, prematurity seems to guarantee an eternity of wariness. It's not so much that you expect the worst, just that you never settle in to trusting that the best will last. Still, after eight years, the Londners had moved beyond the constant worry about death that shadows many parents of premature infants. There were plenty of other things to worry about.

Yet for one so young, Michael seemed to have an uncanny understanding of life's larger issues. Ronnie remembers listening in on the monitor in her sons' bedroom one night and hearing Mikey and Teddy discussing the differences between Christians and Jews, the war in El Salvador, and black holes in outer space. Then Ronnie heard Mikey tell his brother, "You know what, Teddy? I love you." Teddy replied, "Don't die." Mikey answered back, "I have to die."

Six weeks later, in February 1990, Michael awoke with a terrible headache. His parents rushed him to the pediatrician, then to the hospital. No one could figure out what was wrong. A CT scan showed nothing out of Michael's ordinary profile. Without warning or cerebral pressure, Michael's brain herniated. It burst, killing him. Doctors have theorized that the cyst caused by his brain bleed soon after birth put sudden, intolerable pressure on Michael's brain stem. At age eight, he became a neonatal mortality statistic. As Ronnie has noted, even the survivors don't always make it.

For a time, Ronnie was not so sure she would make it either. In a letter to Mikey six months after his death, she wrote that she would eagerly change places with him. "But I would have made a deal for you first," she wrote. "The deal would have been that you wouldn't be handicapped, and that your brother and sister would live long, healthy lives with you, and that your father would remarry a nice woman so you could have a good stepmother." But there was no one to make a deal with.

Losing Michael made Ronnie feel "like the earth split beneath me and swallowed me up." She cried such huge, wracking sobs that her stomach hurt. She was in so much pain, for so long, that she forgot what feeling good was like. Her health and fitness deteriorated. She ignored a bad cough and developed pneumonia. She lost weight, then gained it. She tired easily. Often she would walk into a room with no idea why she was there.

There were further cosmic insults: a hurricane that blew half their house apart, a miscarriage one week later. Ronnie was a zombie when a friend persuaded her to attend a yoga class. Something inside her burst in the first class, and on the way home she cried the whole way. The tears were healing. Soon, during the relaxation period that closed each class, Ronnie could almost feel her body drift away. She began to think she could touch Mikey, and could almost feel his cheek against hers.

And then it all came together for her. In order to be stronger mentally and emotionally, she would also have to be stronger physically. Six months into her yoga regimen, she joined a women's baseball league. She played catcher, relishing how the here-and-now aggressiveness of that position allowed her to push her grief aside just for the moment.

Londner's gym membership included three free sessions with a personal trainer and she graduated to bodybuilding. She

After the Darkest Hour

balked at first, dismissing a private trainer as an affectation of the rich. But soon she was expertly doing bench presses, pull-ups, pull-downs, squats, and lunges. She cried sometimes, but learned to wipe off her face as though she were just sweaty. As her body strained to lift heavier weights, she wrote, "My soul's heavy burden of grief became easier to shoulder. The strength of my muscles has somehow enabled me to carry my anguish with my head up." This became an essay called "How Bodybuilding Rescued Me from Grief." Recently Londner was certified as a personal trainer. She hopes to work with disabled children.

Yes, of course there are times when, she says, "I am still overwhelmed and knocked breathless with longing for my little son." But in making herself stronger, Ronnie Londner has once again discovered moments of pure joy. Recently, while jogging, "I rounded a corner and came across a hedgeful of red and gold hibiscus flowers in full bloom. A citrus tree nearby added its sweet scent." As Ronnie ran on, she felt strong, and deeply appreciative of the beauty around her.

MICHAEL DONALD LONDNER
1981–1990

Grief is in itself a medicine.

—William Cowper, *"Charity"*

16: The Club

It was my mother, bereft at having lost her only granddaughter, who pointed out that now we were part of the club.

"What club?" I wondered.

My mother is a woman of few words, all of them straight to the point.

"The club that no one wants to join," she said.

It's a depiction I've heard more than once since then, and it's as good a description as any of what it feels like to lose a child. The membership requirements of this club are anything but enviable. You have to have felt the floor dropping out and the sky falling in, all in one awful, unthinkable day. You have to have wondered whether you would be able to figure out which shoe to put on which foot, and then wondered why you should bother anyway. You have to have cringed, and perhaps silently flared, when all those people who meant so well said such incredibly inappropriate things to you. You have to have believed you were the first person in the history of the planet ever to feel so empty.

And then later, you find out that other people have felt this way, too. You find out that they have survived, but that they—like you—have survived only as changed people.

Like you, they know there's no going back. You may look exactly like the old you, but you're a different person now. Grief of this magnitude changes you.

The very word *grief* carries heavy baggage. "Stop giving me so much grief!" people say, when what they mean is, "Get off my case," or "Quit your complaining."

Grief makes people uncomfortable. It scares them. They fear it is contagious, and they want to avoid it. A San Francisco woman recalls the "dear friend" who took her aside at her son's funeral and warned, "Don't hang around with the grievers. They'll suck you into their club and never let you out." The admonition was chilling. Who wants to be vacuumed into some society of perpetual sorrow? But it turns out that the club is not just a bunch of chest-beating, hair-pulling half-humans with hollowed cheeks and haunted eyes. It's people who gravitate to one another because, as the San Francisco woman later discovered, "no one else understands." It's also one large group of people: men and women of all ages, races, religions, economic levels, and geographic locales. In the mid-1990s in America, close to 100,000 children die each year—almost 2,000 per week. Violence, disease, accidents, and other sudden disasters claim these young lives. So do the ravages of drugs and other painful indicators of the complicated, difficult times we live in.

Many of these parents would agree that grief's dreary reputation may be well-earned. But they might also say that grieving is not always an entirely melancholy experience. This is not a club whose anthem is "Oh woe is me." By the same

146   *After the Darkest Hour*

token, it's not exactly a cruise ship that any sane person would eagerly sign up for. No one in this club would pretend that mourning is a fine form of recreation. We do not cheerily walk up to each other and chirp, "Good mourning!" But what almost anyone in the club will agree on is that grief can integrate itself into a person's life. It does not have to be the enemy.

Not that grief is supposed to be your best friend, either. But it can become unterrifying. Faced squarely, it demystifies—like almost any other demon in life. Grief can become something that is simply there, not something that makes you want to flee whenever you think about it.

After Emily died, I found myself talking to many, many people in this club that none of us wanted to join. It seemed that its emissaries were everywhere, often where they were least expected. They were seated next to me on airplanes, perfect strangers who happened to get the aisle seat when I was assigned the middle seat. They were at dinner parties, all dressed up, looking elegant, and not at all like the kind of people who planned to suck me into anything. They were in the waiting room at the mechanic's, while all of our cars were having oil changes or lubes. They were everywhere, looking remarkably like normal people, but bearing a special level of awareness.

Even today, we recognize each other's gazes, almost as if we have some secret handshake. We trade tragic tales, but matter-of-factly, as if we are discussing gardening hints or the weather. Sometimes, we share gentle hugs, even as people who do not really know one another. We nod in recognition of certain universal elements of grief. We never, ever offer blanket lines of comfort. We never utter the truisms we have all heard too often. We never spew out those vapid phrases: "There, there, it will be all right". . . or, and this one makes me shudder because it is so fundamentally, so ridiculously untrue, "It's probably better this way". . . or—another shudder—"At least you had him/her as long as you did." We know by intuition and by experience that "it" will never be "all right." We know it couldn't possibly be better this way. And no matter how long we had our son or daughter, it wasn't long enough.

Sometimes, I find myself rolling my eyes in amazement, because what we are saying to one another has such a strong common foundation. It is something intangible that the professional "experts" know less about than we who have stumbled through the tundra of grief. Incredibly, we occasionally smile or even laugh out loud at the cruel absurdity of what so many of us have been through.

And this is when we in the club begin to take stock of the lessons that the mourning process can impart. This is when we begin to understand that while the death of a child will never, ever make sense, we may begin to comprehend the constructive aspects of grief and mourning.

All clubs have certain bylaws, codes of conduct, membership rules, and the like. This club—the club that has no name, but has far more members than any of us would wish—is no exception.

Visible evidences of grief were present throughout the month of June. I report without the slightest degree of shame that there was not a single day in those first three months without tears. I was able a little later to go several days at a time without such overt expressions of emotion, but then, without warning, the waves would sweep over me once again.

—Arthur W. Mielke, *"Through the Valley"*

ADAM VASQUEZ

Adam Vasquez was in the middle seat, the position most parents instinctively think of as safe. He was wedged between his brothers Paul and Stephen, all of them securely strapped in place, or so their mom and dad believed. The accident happened at night on March 27, 1993, not five minutes from the Vasquezes' home outside Dallas. At a speed of sixty-five miles per hour, a giant Chevy Suburban jumped a median strip and plowed straight into their Toyota. It hit with such force that no one remembers feeling anything. But all of a sudden, the truck was on top of their car.

At first the whole family sat there in a daze. The impact was so powerful that Tina and Jesse Vasquez initially assumed that they and their three children must all be dead. Once Tina and Jesse realized they were alive, they heaved a sigh of relief. Sitting in the front seat, they had taken the brunt of the collision. If they had survived, surely the children had fared no worse. But there was little time to think about how lucky they all were, and even less time to thank the fates. Tina stole a glance outside the car window. The ground was on fire, and the flames were moving fast in their direction. Bystanders were racing to pull the Vasquez family from their vehicle. It was all happening with dizzying speed.

A stranger was standing beside Tina's window. "Unlock the car and get out. Fast," the stranger was saying. But Tina was in shock. She had no idea what the words meant.

The driver of the Suburban rapped on Jesse's window and said something, too. With the window rolled up, Jesse could not tell what he was saying. Nor could he smell the breath of this man who had just slammed into them. If he had smelled it, he would remember, because it was two times the legal limit for inebriation.

Policemen yanked the family out just in time. Tina and Jesse were dragged in one direction, away from the fire, their children in another direction. Tina felt a confusing rush of emotions. She believed all three of her sons to be fine. Yet in her heart, there was a vast sensation of loss. That feeling terrified her. All she wanted was to be close to her family. She was screaming, screaming for Adam, although she was not quite sure why.

Just three weeks before, Adam had celebrated his sixth birthday. At eleven, Paul's skin was alabaster white, his hair bright red. Eight-year-old Stephen was swarthy, with black hair and a dusty complexion. Adam had pale, creamy skin, brown hair, and enormous brown eyes. His smile was immense. Adam's mother thought there could not have been a happier child, ever. As the youngest child, Adam was known to everyone as "Baby." "Go and get your Baby," Tina would say to Paul or Stephen, and off they would toddle to get little Adam.

Adam knew he was loved, knew he was the center of the Vasquez family. And no one begrudged him that position. They all just loved him to pieces.

Now the two older boys were watching as someone performed CPR on their Baby. In the car, right after the crash, Stephen saw Adam's head resting on Paul's shoulder. Isn't that amazing? Stephen thought. Baby slept through the whole thing. But if Baby was just asleep, Stephen wondered, why was someone pumping on his chest?

At Parkland Hospital, Tina drifted in and out of consciousness. "Mama," she kept hearing the older boys repeat. "Don't go to sleep." They were afraid that if she closed her eyes, she would never wake up. Through the haze in her head, Tina heard the doctors talking to Jesse and the boys. She heard big, complicated medical words. She didn't want to talk and she didn't want to listen. But the words came through anyway. "Your little brother is very, very sick," a doctor told Paul and Stephen. Adam had been rushed to surgery. His colon was ruptured. That was the least of his injuries.

Early, early the next morning—a Sunday—Tina was released from the emergency room. A nurse told her to go home and get plenty of rest, because she was going to need it. When the nurse said Adam was in the trauma unit, Tina brightened for a moment. That must mean there's hope, she thought. But standing beside her, her own father warned that Adam was in bad shape. That afternoon, Tina's father took her to her son's bedside. It was the shock of her life. There was her little boy, pale as death, hooked up to tubes. Just hours before he had been laughing. Now his eyelids were fluttering.

In hindsight Tina says she is certain that was not her child lying in the hospital bed. "He died the night of the crash," she believes. But his body lingered, to suffer. Adam had massive, traumatic brain damage. His spinal cord was smashed. Pneumonia was flooding his lungs. Adam's condition was too fragile even for doctors to permit him to be turned over. After four days, they told the Vasquezes there was no hope of recovery. Tina was devastated. She was also horribly confused. Part of her thought the doctors were giving up on Adam, saying "oh well, here's another child, let's just pull the plugs on him." But somewhere deep in her soul, she knew this was the right thing, that she and Jesse and Stephen and Paul had to let Adam go.

Jesse was still in another part of the hospital. One foot was dislocated. A kneecap was shattered. Tina shuttled between the beds of her son and husband. And she prayed, looking for guidance. An answer came swiftly. "The main answer from the very start was that given the results of what had happened to Adam, we had to release him from life supports," Tina remembered. Jesse, who had not seen his youngest son since the accident, was less convinced. "I had to literally keep telling Jesse that we had to let Adam go, we had to let him be with the angels, we had to let him go forward," Tina said. "It was very hard."

Jesse was himself released in time to sit with Adam as doctors removed the life supports. "I think it was the Lord's work," Tina said. Tina held one of her son's hands. Jesse held the other. His brothers flanked him as well. Family and friends surrounded him. Once the final tube was removed, "he didn't even last a second," Tina said. Adam was ready to go, Tina believes, and he was relieved to have his parents' blessing.

There are small measures of grace that console Tina and

Jesse when they think about their youngest son's death. Tina is grateful that she and Jesse were beside Adam. She is thankful that his brothers were there as well. She is thankful that Adam loved his family so much, and that he knew how much he was loved by them. When she looks back on those facts, she has no regrets, none at all.

But the ordeal of Adam's death was much greater than what happened at the hospital, or even than what happened when the Suburban hit their car. The driver of the Suburban was taken into police custody immediately after the crash. The next morning he was released, having easily met his bail payment. With Adam's death, he was brought back into custody. Again, he was released pending a trial by jury. Although evidence showed he was legally drunk, the jury was lenient. "They took into consideration the fact that he was young and that he admitted he had a problem drinking," Tina said. "They didn't take into account the fact that there's one less child on this earth because of him."

He served a hundred days in jail, then earned ten years of probation. At the trial Tina said it was all she could do not to reach out and strangle the man who stole her baby's life. Today she tries not to think about him. But when she does, she feels a murderer is walking—driving—the streets.

"I don't put much thought to this guy," she explains. "We've had so much thought about him that it did control our lives. We felt such anger, and of course, we did at times feel the need to get revenge. If I think about it, it angers me. I try not to think about him."

Since Adam Vasquez was killed, the Texas penal code has been changed. Drivers who kill someone while under the influence of alcohol now are charged with intoxication manslaughter rather than involuntary manslaughter. The maximum prison term has been raised from ten to twenty years. For Tina and Jesse, the change offers scant consolation.

The couple has become active in MADD, Mothers Against Drunk Driving. Jesse is one of only two fathers who regularly attend meetings at their Dallas-area chapter. Jesse also speaks before a Victims' Impact Panel that driving-while-intoxicated offenders must attend as part of their probation. Tina meets with new MADD families to try to offer one-on-one support.

For almost a year after the accident, Tina recoiled when Jesse tried to touch her. She was still so angry with him, still blaming him because he had been driving. He was the father, shouldn't he have done something to avert their tragedy? MADD counselors helped Tina understand that many families experience this kind of distance and alienation in the wake of a child's death, whether at the hands of a drunk driver or through other circumstances. And Jesse was persistent. "He didn't want us to end up in the middle of a divorce because we couldn't handle each other's grief," Tina said. "We weren't handling our own too well, either."

As it happens, Adam looked almost exactly like his father. Tina realized she couldn't stand to lose both of them.

Acquaintances clustered around them soon after the accident, but the Vasquezes say they lost friends in the months that followed. Some people said they were grieving too much, as if there were a shelf life on sadness. Others viewed them as what Tina calls "a scarred family—as if, if it happened to us, it could happen to them. They look at us like we're stuck in the past. Nobody talks to us much anymore." And then, of course, some people reminded Tina and Jesse that they are young and that they could after all still have another child. Tina and Jesse know better. "You can't replace one with another," they say.

When they meet new people, they stumble over the how-many-children-do-you-have question. They feel guilty if they exclude Adam, but their questioners squirm if they include him. Tina has had to teach herself not to go in and check on Adam at night. She often has to remind herself that she no longer hears his voice. Even washing the clothes is an adjustment: She's washing for two kids instead of three.

Adam still comes to Tina in her dreams. He tells her she's all right, and that he is, too. In life he was a loving child, always giving kisses. In death it seems he is unchanged.

On frequent visits to the cemetery, the family takes him daisies, Adam's favorite flowers. On his birthday, they release big clouds of balloons for him, straight up to heaven. Tina made him an audiotape with all of his favorite songs, even "Happy Birthday, Dear Adam." When they play that tape, out there at the cemetery, sometimes people look at them like maybe they're a little strange. But Tina and Jesse and Paul and Stephen just huddle very, very close together.

ADAM VASQUEZ
1987–1993

Winter is come and gone,
But grief returns with the revolving year.

—Percy Bysshe Shelley, *"Adonais"*

17: The Unwritten Rules

In that this club has no official roster of members, it also has no rulebook. To my knowledge, no one has ever written a set of regulations, and no one, therefore, has ever been asked to leave the club for failing to adhere to nonexistent policy guidelines. There is no strict code of conduct, no dress rules, and—best of all—given that there isn't much to make light of under these circumstances, no annual dues. But certain precepts are understood. I've tried to compile them, with the stipulation that these maxims are amorphous. There's no one-size-fits-all concept at work here. But at various times in the odyssey of your own grief, it may be useful to realize that certain universal principles apply.

Grief Has No Pride and Asks No Apologies

Grief is never, ever wonderful. No one would be foolish enough to make such an assertion. But it can be good. However, good grief means really giving in to the pain. It means that if you want to cry, you cry. If you want to sob, you sob. If you want to close your bedroom door and pound your pillow while you cry and sob, you do that, too. And you do not have to make amends for this kind of behavior. Pride is not the issue here. Seldom do two different people "do" grief the same way, even when they are mourning the same person. Some people are stony. Others turn into Niagara Falls. The way our club members look at it, it's your grief and you can cry if you want to.

One hint from a veteran of this tear-stained grief front: For many, many months after my daughter died, I drove around with my car windows rolled up, listening to Italian operas at full blast on my tape deck. Opera is replete with tragedy. Someone always dies. That makes it okay to cry, even in traffic.

Grief Can Make You Manic

This is one axiom that probably comes under the heading of "no kidding." In fact, psychologists even have a term for the frenzy that envelopes some people at what logically might seem to be the lowest, most lethargic of moments. They call it "agitated depression," a fancy expression for the fact that you may feel like a gerbil running around in a cage: bouncing off the wall, spinning on your own private roller coaster, racing on a treadmill that never seems to keep up with you.

For example, after my friend Barbara's son David died of Hodgkin's disease, Barbara became a gardening dervish. She had always had a remarkable green thumb, and her garden was a well-earned point of pride. But with David gone, she planted like a mad woman. She ran up huge nursery bills and broke every nail on hands that previously had been manicured once a week. She fired her gardener and did the heavy work, hauling loads of fertilizer that weighed at least as much as she does. All the while, she never stopped crying. It's probably a wonder that her flowers took root—which they did, in wild and glorious profusion—because they were christened with salt water, her tears.

The same psychological professionals who brought us the phrase "agitated depression" might opine that Barbara was engaging in denial or displacement. Quite the contrary. In a burst of botanical fury, she was very firmly giving root to her grief. The flowers blossomed as flamboyant reminders that life lurches on. She even put a name to the object of her energetic attention. She called it David's Garden.

Conversely, Grief Can Zap Every Ounce of Energy

I doubt that scientists have made a study of it, but it may well be that there is no fatigue like the fatigue of grief. Brushing your teeth can seem like the most strenuous exertion imaginable. The mere act of reaching for your shoes in your closet, and then figuring out how to put the left shoe on the left foot and the right shoe on the right foot, may entirely exhaust you.

On those days, it is probably better to forget about brushing your teeth. Plaque is gross, but it is seldom fatal. Besides, it keeps dentists in business. When the dilemma of donning footwear is just too overwhelming, go barefoot. Fashion is not the objective, getting through the day is.

The lesson here is about recognizing and respecting the

precarious quotient of personal energy that comes along with grief. This means marshalling your resources carefully, and realizing that there are some days when you just won't be able to do whatever it is that you thought you "had" to do. More than likely, you will often feel that you have been crushed by a cement mixer. The image is apt: A cement mixer pulverizes your bones. The death of your child smashes your heart to small pieces. The mere act of existence may be all you are up to for a vague and indefinite period of time. Death, it turns out, also drains the living.

What Does a Grieving Parent Look Like?

A grieving mother or father looks like all of us. That is part of the problem. In the olden days, or even today, in far, distant cultures, we would have swathed ourselves in black. Along with our attire, our long faces would have been a signal that this was a different, difficult time. In today's "bounce back" society, we have no such uniform or disguise. This may be one of the reasons we are so vulnerable to the largely innocent but often idiotic remarks people throw out when they see us looking so much like normal people. "You look great!" they announce, assuming apparently that if we look so swell we must be feeling swell, too. One mother recalls standing at the front desk of her pediatrician's office to make an appointment for one of her surviving children. The situation was ordinary enough: toddlers playing with the doctor's cache of well-worn toys, babies screeching, runny-nosed kids assiduously trading germs, frazzled moms looking alternately at the wall clock and their children, wondering just how late the doc was running today.

The mother who told me this story was actually in a zombielike state, two full years after her eight-year-old's death from a cranial hemorrhage. But she was faking it well. A casual observer might have pegged her for serene, not bone-dry empty. The receptionist, who had known her for years and who knew the full story of her family's misfortune, probably thought she was throwing the mother a compliment when she said, "Well, you certainly are more compassionate and patient now than you were before."

"I didn't need my son to die to be compassionate," the mom replied. "I was plenty compassionate before."

The receptionist persisted, as people who think they are being kind often do. "Yes, but this way you are even more sensitive."

Furious and hurt, the mother said nothing more. Later, at the bank, she made a thousand-dollar mistake that was, fortunately, picked up by the teller.

Traveling Incognito

Hiding out does not necessarily mean burrowing into the walls of your own home. Sometimes it feels very safe to be around other people who know nothing about you, nothing about your sorrow. I switched exercise classes after Emily's death. I couldn't bear to go back to a gym where they knew I had been pregnant. I couldn't face the inevitable questions. So I traveled across town, way too far across town, and kicked and jumped and sweated around total strangers. Most of us stared straight at the instructor, no questions asked of one another.

After her son Mikey died of a brain hemorrhage, a friend in Florida signed up for Spanish classes. She loved going to that continuing education program because nobody knew. Nobody knew the secret of her searing pain. She "passed" as normal. But very often she wondered, how many others in that class were doing the same with their secret griefs?

Graveyard Humor

One of the firmest non-rules of our club is that people who have lost children can say anything they want to each other, no judgments offered. This latitude is often a relief, because it allows us an audience for the absurdity of an upside-down universe that claims a child but leaves adults behind. Hospital humor that does not strike other people as funny at all can have us doubled over in bottled-up laughter—which, of course, since our whole world is inverted, is really tears in disguise. We can even make funeral jokes! The sight of grieving parents yakking it up strikes some people as borderline blasphemous. It's as if the fact that we're laughing strips some credibility from our sorrow.

Nothing could be farther from the truth. The pain is real, the sorrow never goes away. But sometimes a moment of merriment is an amazing respite of relief.

Here is an example, provided by my friend Ronnie in Miami, of the kind of thigh-slapper we parents exchange.

Ronnie's surviving son, Teddy, was speaking to his dead brother's spirit: "Mikey, we miss you so much, we need you back with us. Please put your spirit into one of Papa's sperms so you can be in our family again."

"But Bear," said Ronnie, foolishly attempting to insert some reasonableness into the conversation, "how do you know that the sperm Mikey puts his spirit into will be the one that gets to my egg?"

"Mommy! Mikey was a very good swimmer!"

A note of caution: Do not attempt such amusement in the company of your nearest and dearest friends, no matter how sympathetic you believe them to be. Unless they have lived through a comparable experience, they will think you have flipped out, landing in some netherworld of tastelessness. This may not be far from the truth. So when everything is upside down, it may be best to save your jocularity for other people who see the world that way, too, other members of the club that has no name. They are guaranteed to laugh with you. And for a moment or two, that laughter will feel just fine.

Timetables

Grief is a process and it has no timetable. End of subject.

What You "Should" Be Doing

What you should be doing is taking care of yourself, following your own pace. What you should not be doing is feeling drained or discouraged by the expectations of others.

Grief Is Not a Competitive Event

In our club, we know that no child's death is "better" or "worse" than any other child's death. We know that to some people, losing an infant may somehow sound less tragic than losing a twenty-year-old—and that to others, the opposite may be true. We know that how long you had a child is not nearly as significant as the fact that you lost the child. We know that violent death wrenches our souls, but that a so-called "peaceful" death achieves the same end: a child you can no longer hold in your arms.

Again, we learn to grit our teeth and take deep breaths before responding to those uneducated outsiders who may venture an opinion about how "lucky" we were to have a child for a particular amount of time, or how "fortunate" we were not to have "bonded more firmly," or whatever. There is more than enough pain to go around for all of us. Nobody's grief needs to be larger or smaller than anyone else's. Nobody's sorrow needs to be diminished, not for one fleeting nanosecond.

The Secret Society of Grief

At one time in my life I owned a sports car. It was a navy blue convertible, and I loved roaring around in it. Little did I know when I bought it that all the people who owned the same model made a practice of beeping their horns at one another. It was kind of cool, perfect strangers waving and trading happy honks.

There's nothing merry about grief. But the parallel experience is the recognition, the understanding that parents who have lost children unquestioningly extend to one another. There's no secret handshake, brand, or membership pin. But a deep level of awareness makes it possible for us to spot one another.

There's a quiet understanding among us. We're all in this thing together. We didn't choose to be here, but here we are.

Brent Charboneau
Colette Charboneau
Chantal Charboneau

Instinctively, parents who have lost children find one another and draw together. Our common language speeds communication. Never, ever do we play "top this"—as in, "my grief is greater than your grief." We respect without equivocation the sorrow that binds us. Occasionally, however, a story renders special perspective. Here is one. Listen while Dolores Charboneau, a psychologist in Washington, D.C., talks about losing her son, her daughter-in-law, and her granddaughter.

"One of my earliest and most vivid memories is the birth and death of my baby sister. I was about five years old when she was born, and I was delighted to have a baby in the family. Many of our neighbor families had babies, and I was elated that we had one, too. Then, unexpectedly and quite suddenly, the baby died. She was about three months old.

"A child undoubtedly has a limited understanding of death. I grew up always conscious of my little sister's presence. Like the child's view in William Wordworth's poem 'We Are Seven'—in which the child insisted on counting her deceased siblings as part of the family—I counted the sister I had lost. I never considered myself to be the younger of two children. Rather, I saw myself as the middle child in a family of three children.

"When my grieving parents put away the baby clothes and furniture, I was afraid they would erase the memory of her as well. I was afraid they would erase the fact that she had been born at all. The radiance of her smiles, the miraculous sound of her first laugh out loud, her tender new-baby fragrance have remained with me all my life, sweet, precious, and joyful.

"Years later, when I lost my own twenty-one-year-old son Brent and then lost my daughter-in-law Colette and my twelve-year-old granddaughter Chantal, my family and I tried to recover from the horrendous pain and hold on to the sweet, precious, and joyful memories. It has been difficult. Brent and a young companion died at the hands of a drunk driver speeding down the wrong side of the road. Colette and Chantal, the family of my son Michael, were shot by a burglar who broke into their home while they were sleeping. Michael was briefly away at the time, helping his grandfather. Because these three deaths were caused by violence, our pain and anger were multiplied by the thought that our beloved family members were killed by someone who chose to drink and drive, and by someone who wanted to steal what Michael and his wife had worked so long and so hard to build and to acquire.

"My family and I have worked hard to put away the anger and the pain. But sometimes, difficult incidents will shake us up, and cause us to remember once again. An especially troubling incident happened to me about a year after Brent's death. I had previously put away all the reminders of Brent, even photographs. We couldn't bear to see them. Then one day I was in the basement furnace room, where I seldom went, and suddenly felt piercing chest pains. I had always been healthy and had never felt anything like this. Now I wondered if I might be having a heart attack. Then I discovered that when I went to another part of the room, the pains disappeared. But if I went back to the place where they had started, they came right back. After this happened, I noticed Brent's old jeans and tennis shoes. He used to use them for yard work, and had put them in the furnace room before he was killed. I hadn't consciously recognized the clothes as Brent's. But seeing them brought on that tremendous physical pain.

"Losing Colette and Chantal about ten years after Brent's death was torturous for the whole family as we saw Michael suffering so hard over the loss of his own family. He had been a dedicated husband and father, deeply involved with his family for more than fifteen years. He had left them well and happy, only to return, in horror, to find them murdered. He and Colette often worked two or three jobs apiece. They personally built what Colette called their dream house. It turned out to be such a 'success' that a thief killed her and her child in order to burglarize it.

"After the deaths of our loved ones, we found ourselves focused on our grief and our anger. But grief and anger are disabling. We had to move on—move on to be thankful to have had our loved ones as long as we did. We had to heal and move on to take comfort and joy in the happy memories left to us.

"So I treasure my memories of Brent's constant smile, his sense of humor, his protectiveness of his family. He always had a sense of humor, even as a small child. One day, when he was about three years old and still not speaking too clearly, he came in from outside. He was laughing and telling me about the 'at' (cat). I could not understand what the cat had done—but whatever it was, I knew it was funny, so I laughed, too. His humor stayed with him as he grew. One day when he was a schoolboy, he and his brothers were joking with each other, as they often did. A neighbor boy sat down to watch and asked when they were going to put on their skit. Brent was fiercely devoted to his two sisters and three brothers. Shortly before his death, he was leaving home to take a job. 'I can't imagine anything worse than never seeing my family again,' Brent said.

"There are good, rich memories, too, about Colette's kind and loving ways. She never had a bad word to say about any-one. She cherished Michael. When he would tease her, she would laugh and call him a 'pest.' She was artistic, and could sew and design clothes and wall hangings. She spent hours making her wedding dress, carefully sewing on hundreds and hundreds of tiny pearl beads. She had helped to rear her younger siblings, and so as a new mother she had skills and confidence that few new mothers have. Colette worked out-side the home. But for Colette, family and family life came before everything else. In all the years I knew her, I never once heard her use a harsh word.

"Chantal was the first grandchild on both sides of the family. She enchanted us all, and we doted on her. For her baptism, she was decked out like a little princess in the long baptismal gown her mother had made for her, and in the tiny crocheted shoes Michael had worn at his own baptism years before. Chantal was quiet and well-behaved. Often she acted

After the Darkest Hour

older than her years. At about five years of age, she asked for one of the bedrooms on the side of the house overlooking the river, so when she and her college roommate came home for weekend visits, they could 'see the river.' She was already looking way ahead. In the school band, she played the first flute. Michael took such pride in the way her teachers described Chantal as 'the student who always befriended children needing a friend, and the student with whom everyone wanted to be friends.'

"The healing process has not been easy. My family and I still cannot bear to think about the evil that killed our loved ones. But at last the time has come when we can look at the photographs and reminisce about the happy times. Still, we keep the photographs put away so we can prepare ourselves before we see them, and not be surprised when we unexpectedly notice them on a desk or a chest. Every person is unique. There will never be another Brent, another Colette, another Chantal. We will always love them. We will always miss them so very, very much.

"After Brent's death, I went back to school to earn a doctorate in counseling psychology. As a psychologist today, most of my counseling is geared toward the clinically depressed and the bereaved. I know without question that one of the most agonizing experiences any of us will ever have is the death of a child.

"Probably the most obvious reason we are so overwhelmed by a child's death is that the natural order of life prepares us for the deaths of our parents and spouse, but we expect our children to bury us. Another reason is that the role of a parent includes being a protector, keeping a child safe. The child's death can bring not only such feelings of grief, but also feelings of guilt for failing to adequately protect—even though such feelings may not be justified. Even if the child dies as an adult, parents may feel they have failed to protect by failing to caution against illness, accident, or violence. Another issue involved in the death of a child is the loss of hopes and dreams for a life interrupted. Then there is the loss of identity as a parent, the loss of someone to follow the parent, the loss of the continuity of generations.

"As a psychologist, I try to keep advice to a minimum. But there are some commonsense rules that are valuable to the healing process. First, the bereaved parent should talk about the feelings of loss and pain. Second, for some people, medication may be helpful, especially if sleeplessness is a problem. Third, it is important to keep as close as possible to a normal schedule of eating and sleeping. Eating is often difficult, but it is also important at this time to focus on good nutrition. Alcohol is a depressant. Fourth, fresh air, exercise, and light are needed. Sitting in a dark room can bring on depression in people who are not grieving! Fifth, some people are helped by removing photos, clothes, and other reminders until they are no longer painful to see. My experience is that the bereaved who are unwilling to put away reminders are not ready to move on. Sixth, it is necessary to prepare for anniversaries, birthdays, and holidays. Even repetition of the weather on the day the loved one died can be jolting. Seventh, some form of daily recreation which would normally be enjoyable can be helpful to the therapeutic process. Eighth, most people are helped by accepting the hands that reach out to them in the time of sorrow.

After the Darkest Hour

"Grief counseling takes many approaches. As a psychologist, I concentrate on listening to the bereaved express their feelings. The survivors can also sometimes be helped by describing what they would say if they could talk to their loved ones. It can be a great release for survivors to 'talk' to the deceased. Writing letters to the deceased can also be beneficial. Support groups with people who have experienced a similar loss are valuable. Probably one of the greatest aids in the healing process is the belief in an afterlife, and the belief that we will see our loved ones once again.

"I am a mother as well as a psychologist. Most of all, I believe we need to be thankful to have shared the lives of our loved ones."

BRENT CHARBONEAU
November 2, 1954–May 2, 1976

COLETTE CHARBONEAU
May 3, 1949–June 24, 1989

CHANTAL CHARBONEAU
April 28, 1977–June 24, 1989

> *We have suffered only one very severe grief in the death of Annie at Malvern on April 24th, 1851, when she was just over ten years old. She was a most sweet and affectionate child, and I feel sure would have grown into a delightful woman. Tears still sometimes come into my eyes when I think of her sweet ways.*
>
> —Charles Darwin, *The Autobiography*

18: Club Notes

The wisdom of our members is hard-earned, compiled at the highest cost there is. It comes straight from the experience that sets us forever apart.

Not much makes sense after a child's death. Your sense of personal and global equilibrium is shattered. The very notion of reassurance may be elusive when everything you know and value seems upside down, when nothing has reason.

Still, it does seem to make sense to pass on these lessons that we who have lived through a child's death have compiled. Here, then, are some additional points of reference that may help to ease your ache and your sorrow.

Grief Is a Huge, Private Maelstrom

At some point following your child's death, your grief may be so all-encompassing that you wonder how the rest of the world can continue to function. You will marvel that buses are running, telephones are ringing, newspapers are being delivered, and people are eating meatball sandwiches. Meanwhile, you feel that you've been swallowed up by a whirlpool.

Which is true. Because for a time, you have been. Everything is spinning. Even the most normal of everyday activities are overshadowed by the magnitude of your grief. It just does not seem possible that the world could continue, apparently unchanged.

A little girl we will call Rachel died in midsummer. The minor heart murmur doctors detected at her birth turned out to be a major coronary defect. She was four months old when she died.

For months and months afterward, her mother told us, all she could do was cry. The time seemed to pass so slowly, she said. She waited and waited for the nightmare to be over, hoping she would wake up. For weeks she sat in her house, looking out the window and wondering why none of those people outside understood that her baby had died. Even while watching television, she could not figure out why people were going on as if nothing had happened. Didn't they realize that Rachel was dead?

Dizzy and empty—that is how she felt. It took months for her to comprehend that to some extent she would always feel that way.

Solitude

Someone in our club—feeling flippant because if we can't be flippant, who can?—described the need for solitude that many of us experience as "The Garbo Factor." This is when we simply "want to be alone," no questions asked, no explanations offered. This inclination sometimes puzzles people who have not been through the loss of their own child. On an intellectual level, family members and close friends may respect what you insist is a need for uncluttered, unstructured time—time by yourself. But often they fear that if you are alone, you are obsessing, worrying or contemplating who-knows-what. What they may have trouble understanding is that sometimes being alone is imperative. It's instinctual. You need to be away from the fray.

Support

The first and last words on this subject are: Take it where you can find it. If this means hanging around with "the grievers," fine, so be it. Many people derive immeasurable succor from gathering with people who have had experiences on a par with their own. It is a time-tested model.

For mothers and fathers who have lost children, the grandparent of all such organizations is Compassionate Friends, P.O. Box 1347, Oak Brook, IL 60521. A call to the group's headquarters, 708-990-0010, can put you in touch with someone in your area. There are also a number of what might be called topic-specific groups designed to help family members in the wake of particular causes of death, such as murder, AIDS, suicide, SIDS, neonatal death, and drunk driving. You can find a list of some of these organizations at the end of this book.

Another highly user-friendly source of support for many people is the Bible. I spent many hours reading the Psalms to

Emily, and later, when she was gone, to myself. My husband lingers over poetry, a surefire solace for him. "Whatever works" is my advice.

Cleaning House

A hidden benefit of good, old-fashioned grief is what I call housecleaning. I don't mean major, heavily orchestrated scrub-downs—although that may happen, too—and I don't mean cleaning your place of residence. Rather, the detritus of life becomes all too apparent when you are struggling with something so monumental as the death of your child. Often, this means what one father described as "regrouping" in his personal life: that is, dropping the relationships that were no longer helpful, and gravitating toward the people whose comfort he valued.

Rule No. 1, many grieving parents have found, is that anyone who expects you to "snap out of it" probably is not a great person to spend time with just now. Rule No. 2 is that people who do not want you to talk about your grief may not be enhancing your life at this time. Rule No. 3 is that you don't have to explain any of these decisions to anyone. "Right now I need a little space" is all you have to say.

The Other Kind of Housecleaning

We're talking vacuum cleaners, dust-busters, and giant-size bottles of Fantastik here. We're also talking optional, like a noncompulsory class in school. This kind of housecleaning is of special relevance to parents who have lost children because often our children leave behind bedrooms, cribs, play areas, or other material reminders of their young lives. Once again, what you do here is your prerogative. Some parents leave their children's rooms intact. If a glass of water was half-filled on the bedside table, they keep it half-filled, indefinitely. If the bed was left unmade, it remains that way. Others clean up and dust and neaten and straighten, as many parents—especially mothers—do when their children are alive.

Family members and friends may find this behavior strange. Ignore them. They may chasten that it is "healthier" to "put it all away." They are entitled to their opinion, and you are entitled to ignore it.

Some parents genuinely do not want to be surrounded by physical reminders of their children. This is also fine. These parents may want to enlist friends and family members to box and label toys, clothes, books, and other objects. At some time in the future, the parents may want to go through these things.

One piece of advice: When a child dies in the hospital, some friends and family members think they are doing parents a big favor by clearing out all traces of the child before the parents return home. Except in rare cases, this is not true. And the parent who, in a state of numb weakness or acquiescence, accepts such an offer usually regrets it. One compromise is to invite a cherished friend or family member to be with you as you sort through your child's possessions.

Not Cleaning House

Psychologists talk about something called positive adaptation. Often this is used in reference to people who suffer from cancer or other terrible diseases. One psychologist I know has made a study of positive adaptation in disaster victims. She happens to have focused on people who have been through earthquakes or plane crashes. But she might just as well be talking about parents who have lost children.

Positive adaptation basically means making the best of a bad situation. My psychologist friend uses the example of cancer victims who realize anew how important their personal relationships are—and how unimportant the petty distractions of life can turn out to be. Specifically, she found that many women who recovered from cancer stopped caring about housework, because it took precious time away from their families or their friends.

Perhaps this conclusion can be extended to parents who have lost children, as well. Who cares how clean your kitchen really is? Who cares if your windows are sparkling? This is a time to reevaluate. If these activities help you make sense of your sorrow, great. If they seem like invasions on time you would rather spend with yourself, or with someone you care about, forget about them.

What to Say

Talk about learning from experience. There's not a parent among us who has not heard the wrong thing from someone who just didn't know what to say when the subject is a dead child. As time passes, the insensitive remarks probably will not hurt any less. But you may be able to artfully recast the conversation—and in so doing, to instruct the other person in how to address a grieving parent. Should you encounter another parent who is grieving, you will know what that mother or father would like to hear:

"I'm sorry."

"I care."

"I'm so sad for your loss."

"How are you doing right now?"

"What can I do for you?"

"Tell me about your child—I'm here, and I want to listen."

"Here is my phone number. Please call me anytime you feel like talking."

Don't Stop Dreaming

Club members know for a fact that our children often return to us in our dreams. This is not just goofy, wild-eyed wishful thinking. It is not the parents of dead children's counterpart to UFO sightings. It's fact. Sometimes I think they come to check in on us, to see how we're doing. More often, they come to let us know how things are going for them. Club members do not routinely talk about what goes on in these dreams, for fear that even other parents like us may think us a little bit nuts. But when we know each other well, and trust each other; we trade dreams like recipes.

Many of us make a habit of recording these dream-visits. We keep dream journals. Our dreams may be secret and intensely private. But in the right circumstances, we share.

Psychologists say that in any dream there is always one implausible element. Otherwise, even the sanest among us would go crazy without any discernible distinction between dream and reality. In dreams about our lost children, this rule also holds true. A child who was disabled in life may walk in our dreams. Dream-children may scarf down dream-food that they detested in life, vegetables, for instance. Or show up wearing clothes we never bought them.

What matters is that they do show up. These dreams are important. We need them. Don't be afraid of them. Don't hide from them. Don't stop dreaming!

Grief, the Shapeless Presence

Your grief is always going to be there. It doesn't go away. But it does change shape. It shifts around, amoeba-like: large one day and small the next; heavy as lead or icy as steel. Too often it sneaks up on you. Your arms start to ache, for example. You realize at that instant that they ache because they are empty, because it has been too long since you held your child.

Scientists should study the curious properties of grief. For not only is it nebulous, grief has the wizard-like ability to alter its potency. This is one of the amazing qualities of what I think of as good grief, or sometimes, good mourning. It is not that grief suddenly becomes a friendly force or presence. That could never happen. But the very nature of your grief does evolve. It seems to settle in to a nearly comfortable spot. It becomes something you're aware of, not always afraid of.

Here is how the mourning maturation—or maybe mutation is a better word—played out in my house. At first, after our daughter died, my husband and I felt that we were wearing something hard and heavy on our shoulders, all the time. It was a palpable presence. It literally weighed on us, night and day, for weeks and months and years. Then gradually—we still can't put our fingers on just when, or how—something shifted. Now I sometimes feel that I am wearing a soft cape. I will not go so far as to say that this feeling is welcome; there is not one single solitary day when I would not of course prefer to have my child in the flesh than some invisible substitute. But the oppressiveness has vanished. These days, I sometimes feel that this soft shawl is embracing me, as gently as a baby blanket spread around my shoulders. There's a warmth there, the kind of comfort a mother feels when she holds her child close.

My husband feels it, too. Sometimes, when I rub his back, it's as if a friendly, fleeting visitor is with us. It is Emily, of course, an angel who has never fully left us—and who we hope never will.

Epilogue

FINALLY

One day, quite astonished, C. S. Lewis wrote in "A Grief Observed" that "something unexpected has happened." Lewis was referring to the heavy sorrow that had plagued him since the death of his wife. But since there is some universality to grieving over anyone we love so deeply, it seems to me that his experience has resonance for those of us who have lost children as well.

What took Lewis by surprise was the sudden feeling, "almost better than memory," of a deep and unmistakable impression of his wife. It was instantaneous, and Lewis wrote, unanswerable. This powerful image occurred early in the morning, when the light was low and, Lewis confessed, when his mourning was at a low ebb as well. For Lewis, his wife's likeness was a kind of liberation: "It was as if the lifting of the sorrow removed a barrier."

If we parents are lucky, our sorrow will lift. The barrier will drop. The sun will shine.

Resources

AMERICAN ASSOCIATION OF SUICIDOLOGY
Suite 310
4201 Connecticut Avenue NW
Washington, DC 20008
202-237-2280

Since 1968, this nonprofit organization has helped family and friends who have lost a loved one to suicide find survivor support groups, peer counseling, and other services.

THE CANDLELIGHTERS CHILDHOOD CANCER FOUNDATION
7910 Woodmont Avenue
Suite 460
Bethesda, MD 20814
301-657-8401

This group was founded more than a quarter of a century ago to provide advocacy, support, and information for families and survivors of childhood cancer. It is the largest and oldest pediatric cancer organization in the country.

THE COMPASSIONATE FRIENDS, INC.
National Headquarters
P.O. Box 1347
Oak Brook, IL 60521
708-990-0010

   Founded in England in 1969, this nondenominational, nonprofit organization has been helping families who have lost children via regional support groups in the United States since 1972.

MOTHERS AGAINST DRUNK DRIVING (MADD)
P.O. Box 541688
Dallas, TX 75354-1688
800-GET-MADD (800-438-6233)

   Fathers as well as mothers from all over the country join this well-known nonprofit organization to find solace when a child is killed by a drunk driver.

NATIONAL ASSOCIATION OF PEOPLE WITH AIDS
Seventh Floor
1413 K Street NW
Washington, DC 20005
202-898-0414

   This national advocacy and information group provides peer-to-peer counseling and support, as well as educational materials for people who are "infected and affected" by the HIV virus that causes AIDS.

NATIONAL SIDS RESOURCE CENTER AND CLEARINGHOUSE
Circle Solutions
8201 Greensboro Drive
Suite 600
McLean, VA 22102
703-821-8955

   This group offers a wide variety of publications on SIDS.

PARENTS OF MURDERED CHILDREN
100 East 8th Street
Room B41
Cincinnati, OH 45202
513-721-5683

Following the murder of their daughter Lisa, Charlotte and Bob Hullinger launched this nonprofit group in 1978. Support groups are available around the country, as well as legal advice, a newsletter, grief weekends, and other services.

PEDIATRIC AIDS FOUNDATION
1311 Colorado Avenue
Santa Monica, CA 90404
310-395-9051

While primarily focused on fund-raising for AIDS research, this group also provides bilingual education and information material, including videotapes for parents of children with AIDS. This foundation also serves as a referral agency for parents who wish to connect with other parents. It was founded in 1988.

PREGNANCY AND INFANT LOSS CENTER
1415 East Wayzata Boulevard
Wayzata, MN 55391
612-473-9372

Along with a parent-to-parent outreach program, PILC offers educational materials, a newsletter, and information on counseling services. PILC can also connect parents with national and international support groups.

RTS BEREAVEMENT SERVICES
La Crosse-Lutheran Hospital
1910 South Avenue
La Crosse, WI 54601
608-785-0530, ext. 4747

Formerly known as Resolve Through Sharing, this program provides information on local and national support groups for families who have experienced miscarriage, stillbirth, or neonatal death.

SHARE
(A Source of Help in Airing and Resolving Experiences)
St. Joseph's Health Center
300 First Capitol Drive
St. Charles, MO 63301
314-947-6164

This national, nondenominational organization offers support for parents after the death of a baby. The group publishes a newsletter and provides a forum for parents wishing to express their feelings. Information on parent-support programs around the country is also available.

SIDS ALLIANCE
National SIDS Foundation
1314 Bradford Avenue
Baltimore, MD 21208
800-221-SIDS

Parents who have lost a child to sudden infant death syndrome can obtain information, counseling, and referrals through this foundation. Literature, films, and community education packets are also available on SIDS, infant death, and apnea.

SIDS EDUCATIONAL SERVICES INC.
2905 64th Avenue
Cheverly, MD 20785
301-773-9671

In addition to coauthoring *The SIDS Survival Guide*, Joani Nelson Horchler started this informational outreach program for families who have lost a child to sudden infant death syndrome. The focus is on the unique issues presented by a loss to SIDS.

The author gratefully acknowledges permission to reprint the following materials:

Poem by Eleanor Wimbish: Reprinted by permission of the publisher, Random House, Inc.

Afterword by Frances Gunther: Reprinted by permission of the publisher, HarperCollins Publishers, Inc.

Excerpt from "The Friend We Have Not Yet Met" by Joan Walsh Anglund: Copyright © 1993 by Joan Walsh Anglund. Reprinted by permission of Random House, Inc.

Account by Joani Nelson-Horchler: Reprinted by permission of the author.